MW00780056

Upside-Down, Inside-Out, and Backwards Marketing

Upside-Down, Inside-Out, and Backwards Marketing

**THE SUPRISINGLY LOGICAL FORMULA FOR MASSIVE
GROWTH OF YOUR SALES AND PROFITS**

Bernie Heer

Copyright © 2015 Bernie Heer
All rights reserved.

ISBN: 0692394400
ISBN 13: 9780692394403

Table of Contents

Preface

Business as Usual Is Dead

Let's face it: most advertising and marketing done by contractors is awful.

Incredible amounts of money are wasted on ineffective advertising. No one really knows the difference between a "good" ad and a "bad" ad. Even fewer can figure out why their websites—which they spent untold hours and dollars to put up—aren't generating the flood of customers they were promised they would.

Most ads are designed by simply copying what everyone else in your particular segment of the contracting industry is doing...which was copied from someone else before. Ad reps have no clue how to create an ad that really works, so they do the same thing...copy other ads. The result is that everyone looks the same to the buyer.

Is that what you wanted your advertising to accomplish? Is that why you're spending a pile of money on marketing and advertising every month?

If you opened this book because you wanted to find a magic bullet to attract more customers and make a lot more money, then you're in the right place. (After all, the cover says that's what you will find in these pages, so I'd better deliver!) This book will open your eyes to an entirely different way of marketing, one that is unlike what you've done in the past *and* what you're doing now.

Let me start with some definitions. First of all…

What the Heck Is "Marketing" Anyway?

Good question, glad you asked.

My definition of marketing is this: everything you do to generate and keep customers for your business.

Generating customers—to me—includes not only your advertising that delivers leads to you but also your sales process. That's the first bit of *backwards* advice I'm giving you: marketing and sales should be thought of as one process.

Now, most definitions of marketing stop right there—at generating customers. By adding the requirement that your marketing also needs to work at keeping your customers, we add an entirely new dimension, one—it turns out—that's the keystone to success and riches in your contracting business.

If you're in the type of business that you think only serves customers once—like custom home building, home remodeling, pool and spa contracting, roofing, and so forth—please don't abandon me just yet. I think you'll agree, once you've read this book, that keeping your past customers engaged with you is a darned good idea.

One more thing,,,when I speak of marketing, I mean advertising as well (plus a whole lot more). So, from here on in, I'm no longer going to say "advertising and marketing." I'm just going to say "marketing," and you'll know that I mean advertising as well.

Looking back, there may have been a time when the contracting business was easy. There were plenty of people spending big bucks on additions, new homes, new paint every two or three years, and elaborate landscaping installations. They were putting in pools and hot tubs, and everybody had plenty of work. But that's a distant memory, isn't it?

The world has changed. No longer is money flowing as freely as it once did. There is a sense, even among the affluent, that spending money like there's no tomorrow isn't fashionable anymore. Getting customers to part with their money is harder and harder all the time.

And being "good" is no longer good enough. You can be the very best practitioner of your trade, offer the very highest quality, deliver over-the-top results for your customers, work sixty hours a week to make sure everything is done just so…and still darned near starve to death.

These days, the *minimum expectation* is that you do a superb job. You have to push harder than ever. You have to delight and astonish your clients in order to keep your head above the water. It is definitely *not* business as usual.

But you have to market yourself. You see, it's like this…

If No One Is Buying Your Services… You're Dead in the Water!

The question, then, is how you will go about marketing yourself.

In the chapters that follow, I will lay out a plan for you that's radically different from anything you've likely seen or done before. And yet the strategies that I'm handing you are as old as selling itself. While they have been proven again and again over the course of time, they remain hidden from so many.

You'll see that upside-down, inside out, and backwards marketing really is the most logical approach to lasting business success.

You will no longer be content to do copycat ads like all of your competitors do. Traditional marketing will turn you off. It'll be *your turn* to tell the Yellow Pages rep or the radio sales gal or the website designer what to do—not the other way around. Your eyes will be opened to a fresh new way of marketing that's not only lucrative but fun too.

This book is your navigator to riches. You *can* recapture the dreams you once had for yourself and your business.

What's Inside?
Section I – Upside-Down Marketing

This section is a crash course on the fundamentals behind these marketing concepts. While I know it's tempting to skip this section, it's critical that you understand the logic and thinking that underlie the specific strategies.

If you fail to grasp these, you will lack the foundational knowledge, and you will almost certainly not be able to properly apply the marketing methods contained in the other sections.

And then you'll blame your failure on me…which I cannot allow.

Section II – Inside-Out Marketing

In this section, we explore how to show the outside world the inside reality of your company. There's a new movement in marketing—especially online—that's called "inbound marketing." It's all about attracting prospects by letting buyers have a peek inside your business.

I hate to say this, but direct marketing has been using these methods for over one hundred years! They're nothing new, just a new name and a new wrapper.

The good news is that they work, and I've adapted these ideas and refined them specifically for the building and contracting industries.

Section III – Backwards Marketing

These chapters focus on the specific strategies that you can use in your business to double or even triple your leads, sales, revenues, and profits.

Here you will find ideas that will translate directly to your business. Take these concepts, copy them, and apply them in your business. Then watch as your bank account swells.

I call these "backwards" strategies because we approach them in a very different way than just about anyone else does—and hard data has proven that my way is better.

I know you're most interested in this chapter, but please do me one favor: don't skip the first two sections and only read the third. Without the thinking and logic behind the strategies, they will not work nearly as well for you, and they may even fail completely.

Section IV – Applying Upside-Down, Inside-Out and Backwards Marketing Strategies

In this section I show you how to take the strategies we've talked about and quickly apply them to your business to generate amazing increases in your sales and profits.

Let's dive in and go upside down!

SECTION I
Upside-Down Marketing

CHAPTER 1

Marketing That Provokes a Response

In this chapter we'll begin to lay the foundation that will earn you top profits in your contracting business.

But before we get to that, you might wonder how I came to write this book. Who am I to give advice to anyone on the topic of building a business…getting more clients…making more money?

I think a bit of introduction is required here. After all, you want to know whether your time will be well spent with this book and whether my writings will be worth your time in reading.

Here's my story…

I have stood in your shoes. I've owned businesses and had slumps. I've sat in my office wondering why the phone wasn't ringing, doubting whether anyone was ever going to call again.

I've emptied my bank account to run an ad, desperately hoping that it would pay off. It returned break-even…at best.

I've faced that cold telephone…made the dials…endured the soul-crushing rejection…day in and day out. It's humiliating. In one two-month period, I made 2,437 dials—I kept the records, you see. I spoke to 123 people, got six appointments, and made one sale…a small one.

That hurt.

The website that promised a huge return was a flop…no traffic. I was told I needed to do SEO…more money…still showing up on the third page of Google.

Pay per click, I was advised, was the way to go. It was not. I paid, but the clicks didn't buy.

"The key," they said, "is to have videos on your website and have them posted on YouTube so that people can find you." No one found my videos…or me.

"You need to get a mobile site." Got one…didn't change anything.

Facebook…no friends…

Twitter…no followers…

LinkedIn…no links…

Trust me. I've been there.

Finally, I decided that it was *up to me* to figure out how to get paying customers to call me. After all, there were others in my industry that I knew were making tons of money, yet throwing my hard-earned dollars at the "expert" advertising salespeople and Internet "gurus" wasn't making it happen for me. All I was doing was making *them* rich!

So I went to the bookstore one day at lunchtime and went to the business section. There were two huge shelves filled with business books.

Which of these would help me the most? By luck, I picked up a book on direct marketing.

I must say that I was feeling pretty low at that point, and I didn't really think this book was going to help me much. But I started reading it in my office that afternoon…and I couldn't stop reading!

Discovering a Hidden World

The methods and strategies outlined in this book were so different, and the thinking behind the ideas so radical to me, it was as if my eyes were opened for the first time. It just made so much sense…Why hadn't anyone ever told me about this kind of marketing before?

I finished that book at about two in the morning, after reading almost nonstop since opening it. Along the way I was rereading whole chapters because I wanted to be sure I didn't miss a single thing. I even read straight through dinner, which didn't please my wife one bit.

The biggest revelation to me was that attracting customers and making money is *not* an imprecise art. In fact, nothing could be further from the truth. I had thought marketing was some sort of "dark magic" that I could never do myself. In actuality, there is a long history of proven techniques and strategies, actions that *you* can take to practically guarantee that your business will succeed.

Boy, was this good news to me!

To make a long story short, I started using the new methods that I'd learned from the book, tailoring them to my business. In no time, the phone was ringing, I was getting plenty of new customers, and my business was humming along nicely.

But I was curious. I wanted to find out *why* these methods work so well. I began to devour everything I could about direct marketing. I became obsessed and spent countless hours—and over $100,000—attending seminars and webinars, joining mastermind groups with other like-minded marketers, and buying every book and manual I could lay my hands on.

I wanted to uncover the keys…figure out the puzzle…unravel the mysteries that make this type of marketing so effective. I studied every direct-marketing guru I could find: the legendary Dan Kennedy, Jay Abraham, Joe Sugarman, Perry Marshall, Ken McCarthy, and others. Copywriters like Gary Halbert and John Carlton. Even the big names in direct marketing from bygone days, like John Caples, Robert Collier, and Claude Hopkins.

At some of the seminars and events I attended, I met incredibly smart and creative marketers. Among them were dentists, carpet cleaners, Internet gurus, authors, chiropractors, motivational speakers, restaurant owners, IT guys, mortgage brokers, retailers, insurance agents, auto mechanics, industrial suppliers, farmers, and, yes, contractors. All of them were using—with great success—the techniques and strategies I have outlined for you in this book.

So I adapted and tested methods I'd read and heard about that I thought would improve my marketing. If they worked, I kept them. If they flopped, I tossed them out.

I ended up with a number of proven strategies to easily and *consistently* bring in new clients. I'm very pleased to tell you that, after using these strategies for over ten years and turning my business into a cash machine, in 2011—at the age of forty-eight—I was able to sell that business for a very healthy seven-figure sum.

I'm happy to say that my house is paid for, my cars are paid for, my son's college fund is full, and I have plenty of money stashed away to secure my retirement. I don't think twice when booking a nice vacation or buying fine things for myself or my family. I've been very lucky, and I'm grateful for all that I have been given.

My mission now is to help other business owners to master the same methods I used so that they, too, can build their businesses, attain financial freedom, and make their own dreams come true.

Okay, enough about me. Let's start digging into these not-so-secret secrets.

The Market-Message-Media Triangle

The truth is that the entire marketing process can be boiled down to just three steps. It's very important that you follow these steps in the order that I have outlined them for you here.

One of the big mistakes that I was making, and so many businesses make, is that I was doing them in reverse order—*upside down*. Getting this right was my first big step toward financial freedom.

Choose Your Market

The first main step is choosing a market that's hungry for what you have to offer *and* can afford your services. That may seem obvious, but so few contractors give it any serious thought.

Chapter 2 is devoted to finding just the right target market *for you*.

Create Your Marketing Message

The second step is crafting a marketing message. In chapter 3 we'll focus on creating the perfect marketing message for your target market. Where most business owners miss the mark is that they fail to put themselves in their prospects' shoes…to understand them at an *emotional* level.

Most traditional marketing methods fail at this as well. I guarantee that once you have a good understanding of the methods contained in this book, you'll look back at your old advertising and smack yourself in the head at how bad it really was.

Choose Your Media

The third step in the marketing process is choosing the methods that you're going to use to reach your target markets. I cover this in detail in chapter 4. This is the third step and *must* be done last.

What Everybody's Doing Wrong

Almost every business does these steps in *upside-down* order.

The first thing they do is choose the media, oftentimes because a sales rep showed up at their door. Or they look at where everybody else in their industry is advertising, and they advertise there too. More on this later.

Once they've chosen the media, then they say, "Hmmm, what should we say in our ad?" Usually they decide to talk about how great they are, how long they've been in business, what services they provide, where their business is located, and so on. Wrong, wrong, wrong.

And most never even get to target marketing, which is really the most important step of all.

Now, a lot of business owners *think* they have a target market, meaning they have some sort of picture in their mind of an ideal customer—or, in today's business-speak, an *avatar*—but these exist only in their imaginations. They're not really doing anything to actively seek them out. They never really consider *where* their message is going to show up and whether it will reach their target audience.

If you're being honest with yourself, I think you'll admit that your own marketing efforts have been handled this way. You're just crossing your fingers that more good customers will show up than the cheapskate customers you seem to attract.

Am I right?

Well, all of that is in the past. And, as I like to say, "You are *not* your past."

In other words, your past need not control your future.

If you're a reputable contractor who cares about delivering quality results for your customers, then I have another little saying for you that I think is fitting: *there's nothing wrong with your business that can't be fixed by what's right with your business.*

It's just a matter of selecting the best audience and getting your message to them using the proper media—in that order.

We're already well down the road toward your success. Let's keep going!

CHAPTER 2

Decide Upon a Market with Strong Potential

There are a couple of things I want you to notice about the title of this chapter.

First, notice that I used the word "Decide." By that I mean that *you* are going to decide who you want to market your services to.

Why? Well, the short answer is that you're going to get customers from the pool of people you market to. That makes sense, doesn't it? So shouldn't you decide who you will send your marketing message to so that you end up with clients you want?

I hope you said yes to that question.

Then I used the words "a Market with Strong Potential."

By that I mean a market where your chances of success are high. For just about any kind of contractor, a neighborhood of newer semi-luxury or luxury homes is clearly going to be more promising than a neighborhood of older modest homes. Yet so many contractors waste money on marketing campaigns that are too broad and reach all types of markets.

If you shrink the number of people you are reaching with your marketing message, you can spend more per person who you hope will see your message. The more specifically you define the inhabitants of your target market, the more you can tailor a marketing message of intense interest to them.

I can't tell you how many times I've heard a contractor say, "My customers are all penny-pinching skinflints…" or "My customers are the *worst*…" or something similar. Well, whose fault is it that they found you? Whose fault is it that you accepted them as clients? It's certainly not *their* fault.

You must determine where the people are—and they are out there—who have the ability to pay and will happily pay premium prices for your services.

Let's take a minute and define what we mean by "markets." Markets are groups of people that have certain characteristics in common.

How to Define Your Market

While the first thing most businesspeople think of is geographic markets—people who live in the same neighborhood or subdivision—there are plenty of other ways to define a market.

A market could consist of people who live in homes of a certain price range. Or people within a specific age or income range. Or people within the same profession, the same political party, people whose kids go to the same private school, people who own collector cars or ride touring motorcycles (but not adventure bikes or sport bikes…Those are different markets).

You have people who like liver and onions, opera lovers, men named Roger who like to play hockey, mothers between thirty-five and forty-five who subscribe to *Cosmopolitan* and carry an American Express card, or those who live in the same style of home.

If you're a remodeling contractor who lives in the Northeast United States and can figure out a way to make the split-level house more appealing, that last one would be a market for you.

There's really no end to the criteria that you can use to define your market.

One of the very best markets, as I will explain in a later chapter, is your own client base.

The vast majority of businesses—including contractors—make the mistake of defining their target markets as "everyone," or even worse, "anyone." I'm convinced that this is *the* major contributing factor that causes more than half of all contracting businesses to shut down within five years of start-up.

You see, it costs a small fortune to reach such a large market. Most contractors spend their limited marketing budget trying to advertise too broadly. They get only minimal response—or maybe no response—because they couldn't afford an ad that pulls well, and then they go under.

Here's what I want you to do to get started. Create a scatterplot for yourself. Get a map of your service area and put a pushpin in everywhere you've had a "good" customer. You will want to get your client list out to make sure you don't leave anyone out.

In chapter 7 I'll tell you about scheduling focus hours for yourself. Spend your first focus hour doing this exercise. If I were you, I'd put a little flag on this page or fold the corner down so that you can come back here.

The result of your scatterplot, I hope, will show you where you might want to focus your marketing efforts to start. At some point, though, it'll benefit you to get a more detailed profile of your ideal customers. What size home do they live in? What kinds of cars do they drive? Where do they shop? What sort of music do they listen to? Where do they go on vacation? Where do they send their kids to school? And so on.

Let me give you a huge hint: you will instantly be more successful if you select a target market that is affluent. Look at the questions in the last paragraph again, and figure out where affluent people in your area gather. What community organizations do they affiliate with—the theater, the symphony, the Rotary Club? Perhaps you can provide services to the theater or the opera in exchange for their mailing list.

Then, once you've identified a target market, you will start "farming" that market. You're going to do that by sending interesting, effective direct-response ads to that market—using various media—over and over again, until you have established yourself as *the* contractor for that neighborhood or market.

Then you move on to the next market you would like to conquer. But you're not going to forget about your first market. You'll continue to nurture it so that a competitor doesn't come along and steal it from you. We're going to cover exactly how to do this in section III.

How to Ruin Your Reputation in Your Target Market...Fast

Way back when I started my first business—which was an employee-benefits consulting firm—I made the mistake that so many new business owners make...I hung out my shingle and started dialing for dollars.

On the rare occasions that I actually ended up talking to someone, I had nothing to offer except what everyone else in my ultracompetitive market was offering. No wonder I wasn't getting much positive response.

I realized pretty quickly that I'd better figure out a way to offer something attractive to buyers that my competitors weren't offering. What I decided to do was put together a package of services that would take virtually the entire burden of health insurance off of small employers. I did everything for them: resolved billing issues, chased denied claims for their employees, handled their regulatory and compliance matters, completed their annual reporting, did a full-blown medical plan marketing every year, and on and on.

As it turned out, this was a pretty smart decision. You see, what I had almost instinctively done was to put myself in my clients' and prospects' shoes and figured out how I could make it easy for them to do business with me. I had adopted a customer-focused approach to doing business.

My clients became raving fans. They loved me. When HR managers I'd worked with left a company, they very often called me soon afterward to ask whether I would work with them at their new company. Their broker didn't provide any of the services that I provided.

I got some very large clients this way, clients that I would never have been able to get by telemarketing or most traditional advertising means.

My advice to you is that you adopt a similar approach. The quickest way to sabotage your efforts to develop a target market is to deliver anything less than absolutely superb results. If you are not committed to providing this level of service and results, the powerful marketing strategies I'm sharing with you in this book will only serve to speed the process by which your target audience figures out that you're no good.

That's not what you want, is it?

I cover this topic in greater detail in section II, especially in chapter 8, where we talk about word-of-mouth marketing. But for now, I want you to understand that you need to put yourself in your prospects' shoes not only when developing your marketing but also in developing your internal processes and how you interact with clients and prospects.

In the next chapter, we're going to figure out how to develop the message that will speak directly to your target market and that you'll use to create the marketing pieces to farm your target market.

CHAPTER 3

How to Capture the Attention of Your Target Market

Have you ever asked yourself this question: What is it that people buy from me?

If you think they're buying a new sunroom, or a pool, or a new roof, or some bushes and plants, or paint, or blacktop, or cabinets and countertop and tile...then I can tell you why your marketing isn't working very well.

If you think they're buying your *experience* or your *professionalism*, then you've missed the mark again. Sure, those things are important to people, but they are not the reason they buy what you're selling. They demand these from every contractor they'll consider doing business with.

People will part with their money for only two reasons:

1. They have a problem and need a solution.
2. They want the benefits and positive feelings they get from the purchase.

In other words, people buy from you because of what your services can do *for them*.

In order to create an effective marketing message, you have to focus on how you will deliver the positive benefits or provide the solution to the problems the inhabitants of your target market face.

So instead of selling remodeling services, you're going to sell comfort, enjoyable family time together, and luxury.

Instead of paint, you're going to sell pride of ownership, prestige, and free time.

You're not going to sell a pool, you're going to sell the pool lifestyle.

Not plants and bushes, but the envy that the neighbors will have.

Not a roof, but beauty and peace of mind.

Not blacktop, but release from the scorn of their neighbors and friends, who look down their noses at your prospect's crumbling driveway.

Do you see the difference?

The Importance of Emotions

Cicero, a very insightful guy who lived a long time ago, said, "If you wish to persuade me, you must think my thoughts, feel my feelings, and speak my words."

I can't think of a better way to say it.

The first step in creating a great marketing message is to understand your target market at an emotional level and connect with them there. You need to laser-focus your attention on what your customers want deep down, and incorporate those points into your marketing message

Let me give you an idea of what people want:

- good health
- more leisure and free time
- more conveniences in their lives
- things that are durable and long-lasting
- a feeling of safety
- things that are cutting-edge or state-of-the-art
- things that will enhance their looks or image—either real or as perceived by others (especially the opposite sex)
- things that make life easier
- more self-confidence

But people don't just want those things. They want to *feel* differently too. People want to

- be respected—or envied—by others,
- be in control,
- be current with style and fashions (even cutting-edge),
- feel proud of their accomplishments,
- have influence over others,
- be recognized as experts,
- be viewed as having accomplished their goals.

Just as important, people want to avoid pain. In fact, the desire to avoid pain is even greater than the desire to experience pleasure!
People want to avoid

- looking foolish or out of place,
- pain or discomfort (both emotional and physical),
- being controlled by others,
- losing money or valued material possessions,
- being embarrassed,
- threats to their current status or possessions.

Think about the effect that a new luxury kitchen or a beautifully land-scaped yard has on the owner's friends, neighbors, work associates, and family members. It ticks a lot of boxes, doesn't it?

Now, if you do kitchen remodels, it would make a lot of sense to get testimonials from your client and send a letter—including references to each and every one of these points—to everyone in the neighborhood, wouldn't it? It's very much like the new car phenomenon: one guy gets a new car, and the next thing you know, every guy in the neighborhood is getting a new car. Now you know why they behave that way.

The Greatest Marketing Skill

There is no greater marketing skill that you can develop than being able to recognize and express your prospects' innermost desires. If there is one master key to creating effective marketing, this is it.

Okay, let's get back to ground level. How do we use this newfound understanding of our target market to make the phone ring and bring in new customers?

We're going to start by creating a unique selling proposition, or a USP. It's not especially difficult to develop your own USP, but it will have a dramatic impact on your business—both internally and externally—and on your revenue and profits.

A USP answers the question all prospective customers have in the back of their minds: "Why should I choose you over any other contractor or any other option I have, including doing nothing at all?"

First, we're going to use what we just learned about connecting with your target market on an *emotional level.* And, in addition to answering why they should choose you, your USP must be very specific and meaningful to your target audience. And, lastly, it has to convey what makes you different and special.

A really great USP makes people ask the question, "Hmmm, I wonder how they do that?"

Go back to the beginning of this chapter and look again at the part where I wrote about what you really are selling. It's not a bad idea to ask some of your good clients why they selected you over other options. You may be surprised at their answers, and you will gain insights.

I wish I could write your USP for you, but I can't. But, let's have a look at a few examples that might be helpful to you in getting a start.

Let's say that you're a home remodeler, and your target market is upscale neighborhoods. Your USP might be "Luxury Home Additions Customized Just for You."

A different spin on this would be "Affordable Luxury Home Additions Customized Just for You."

Can you feel the difference between the two?

Another angle could be "Custom Luxury Home Additions by Master Craftsmen...Completed in Thirty Days or Less...Guaranteed."

That would certainly get people asking, "Hmmm, I wonder how they do that?"

One other point I'd like to make about USPs is that you can have more than one. A painter might have one USP for interior painting and a different one for exterior. That would be smart, in fact.

Get the Word Out

Now, it's not going to do you any good at all to have a great USP—one that you've carefully shaped to appeal directly to your target market's emotional needs—unless you do something with it. But what to do?

Well, you could put it on the side of your vehicles.

You could make yard signs that include your USP. (And please, build yourself a nice yard sign. You are a contractor, after all. Don't use one of the flimsy signs that the politicians use.)

You could start using your USP in your advertisements. You see, your USP is as much about repelling people who are not in your target market as it is about attracting those who are. If you've taken my advice and are targeting an affluent market, I think you'll agree that people from less-affluent areas won't bother to call if your ad specifies that you build "Luxury Swimming Pools and Hot Tubs for Discerning Homeowners."

You could get on the phone and call your accountant, dentist, insurance agents (all of them…your life insurance agent, your benefits broker, your business insurance agent, your auto and home agent, etc.), veterinarian, payroll company owner, menswear store owner, bank manager, lawyer, your kids' karate teacher, the owner of the restaurant where you get pizza every Friday night, the Realtor you bought your house from, and on and on. The purpose of your call is to invite them to breakfast or lunch. (I prefer breakfast because it's usually less expensive, and people's heads aren't clogged up with the day's problems.)

Simply call these folks up—after all, you are a client of theirs—and explain that you'd like to buy them breakfast and tell them a little more about the kind of work you do. Let them know that you're not trying to get them to buy anything—in fact, you would be surprised if they were even in the market for your services. You just would like them to know more about your company and the type of work you do.

Over breakfast, tell them about your USP. I promise you none of these people knows for sure exactly what you do, who your ideal client is, or why you're different from any other contractors they know in your industry. As a very successful sales pro once told me, It's hard for people not to listen to you when they have your sandwich in their mouth.

I wouldn't be especially surprised if you found that at least one of them has a friend, neighbor, colleague, or family member who happens to need your services right now. Or maybe *he or she* needs you.

That, by the way, is called *hustle*. It's old school, and it's not fashionable. These days, most business owners—and most contractors—would rather sit in their offices or shops waiting for their websites and their "social media strategies" to magically deliver all of the prospects they could possibly hope to have.

Bad news…it ain't likely to happen.

There are any number of ways to get the word out about your USP.

To create a strong marketing message, follow these steps:

1. Start by understanding the deepest desires of the people that make up the market you are targeting.
2. Create your message by focusing on their unfulfilled desires.
3. Make sure your ads contain benefits instead of features and will appeal to your audience's emotions.
4. Construct your message to provide a solution to a problem or to hit an emotional trigger.
5. Speak of end results and feelings.

Follow these pointers, and watch as your marketing results climb higher and higher.

PS: My own USP is this: "I offer customized tools to contractors that drive massive increases in sales and profits…guaranteed."

CHAPTER 4

Getting Your Message Out There

In the last chapter, I gave you a few ideas about how to get your USP out into the marketplace. But getting your USP out there won't, by itself, generate enough interest from your target market to keep client flow where you need it to be.

You're going to need to use other channels to market and advertise, and the list of media that you can choose from is long. Even a "short" list would include the following:

- newspaper (both daily and the free weekly community papers we all get)
- radio
- Yellow Pages
- outdoor advertising (billboards, bus stop benches, etc.)
- Valpak
- church bulletins
- telemarketing
- publicity
- home shows and exhibitions
- sponsorships (both specific events and sports teams)
- promotional products
- TV
- postcards
- sales letters
- holiday cards

- vehicle lettering and wrapping
- restaurant place mats
- blimp sponsorship

And, of course, there are the Internet-based strategies:

- website (properly optimized for your keywords)
- e-mail
- search engine optimization (SEO) and search engine marketing (SEM)
- pay-per-click campaigns
- social media (Whole books have been written about each of these channels.)
- Craigslist
- Angie's List
- HomeAdvisor and other similar web-based referral services

And there are plenty more options. It's easy to go broke trying out different media. Where to start?

Well, first of all, I want to start by suggesting that you change your entire mind-set about how you advertise. Of course, my way is upside down from the way every other contractor is thinking about this.

Upside-Down Strategies to Get Your Message into the Market

It's discouraging to me to see the poor advertising and marketing being done in our industry. It all looks and sounds the same. It's hard to tell what one offers that's any different or better than what another offers.

They all use the same old clichés: "Family Owned and Operated," "In Business Seventeen Years," "Third Generation," "Satisfaction Guaranteed," "Customers Are Our Number One Priority," or the one I hate the most, "It's What We Do" (as in "Paving...It's What We Do"). Ugh!

What does that even mean? I could say, "Pooping…It's What I Do." Who cares? The money wasted is practically criminal.

I'll bet that if you pulled up your own website and then pulled up your most-hated competitor's website, the messages would be essentially the same. Go ahead…open them up right now. Ignoring the design elements of each site for a moment, if you switched out the logo and company name, don't they send essentially the same message to the visitor?

Yikes! Is that why you're spending a small fortune on your website?

And the same goes for Yellow Pages ads, newspaper ads, e-mail campaigns, and on and on. So, clearly, you need to do something different.

Let me ask you a question.

Let's say for the moment that you've given up your contracting business, and your new business is baking and selling cupcakes. You sell all kinds of cupcakes, but you specialize in gluten-free cupcakes, which are priced higher than regular cupcakes and are much more profitable for you.

You've been invited to visit your local elementary school for a career day, and you've just finished showing the pupils how you decorate your cupcakes. There's a big group of kids in front of you, and you say, "Kids, I've got a whole bunch of delicious cupcakes here of all kinds, including gluten-free cupcakes. Now, each of you is going to get one, but who wants a gluten-free cupcake?"

Who is going to raise their hands? That's right…your target market.

Now, how does that translate to marketing your contracting services?

Very simple. You see, the children raised their hands because you offered *something created especially for them*. All you need to do is create something of interest to your target market, ideally something created just for them, and allow them to raise their hands.

Crafting the Message for Your Target Market

If you've decided to target a neighborhood of nice homes that were built sixty years ago, your message would be quite different from the contractor who is targeting homes built within the last ten years. That makes sense, doesn't it?

What I suggest you do, as a start, is position yourself as the contractor who is on the consumer's side. You're going to help them understand—teach them—about your industry, your processes, and what goes into a project to deliver the quality end result that they want. In short, you're going to educate them about how to select the right contractor *for them*.

Before we get to that, we need to talk about price competition for a moment.

Look, people who set out to hire a contractor to perform a job—whether it's painting their home, putting on an addition, remodeling their kitchen, putting in a pool, updating their landscaping, installing new siding and windows, or whatever—start out with price. Right? The very first thing they ask themselves is, "How much is it going to cost us to get this project done?"

So, unless you are the low-priced contractor in your area—and I hope you're not—you have to deal with the price issue. You can't go into a bid-presentation meeting unprepared to address the price issue, because it's there... every time. You have to prepare yourself for *when* it comes up, not hope that it doesn't. In fact, if price doesn't come up, you're probably not getting the deal.

You have to begin the process of overcoming the price objection from the very start of your interaction with prospects. And the very first contact they have with you is an ad they see, a mailing you've sent them, a search engine result that they can click on, a Google+ Local page, or your website (which they've visited to check you out after they saw your truck or your yard sign, or their neighbor recommended you).

Yes, that's right…In their first contact with you, you aren't even there. So you'd better be absolutely certain that your ads, mailings, websites, on-line directory pages—everything—send the message that you want them to receive.

And that message should be "I'm on your side."

You deliver that message by offering information that you've produced just for them. If I asked you to create a consumer education piece—a report of sorts—entitled "Twenty-Seven Secrets to Planning the Perfect Kitchen," could you do it? I expect you could.

How about "The Twenty-Five Questions You Absolutely, Positively *Must* Ask Every Contractor Before Selecting One to Install Your New Pool"? Could you write that?

Or "Don't Make These Mistakes When Hiring a Painter…Confessions of a Professional Painting Contractor"?

"How to Hire a Great Roofing Contractor…and Avoid Making a Choice You'll Later Regret"?

You establish right from the start that you're different than all the other contractors out there. You're giving consumers a peek inside your industry so that they can make better decisions on an expenditure that is probably going to be pretty significant for them. And you're going to give them this information without any obligation to hire you—or even speak to you or meet with you.

Do you think that would position you positively in their eyes?

And there are other benefits to this type of marketing as well. Who do you think is going to request the consumer guide that you've written? Of course, it's the people who are thinking about doing a kitchen remodel or having their house painted or having a pool installed or having their roof redone.

Once they've raised their hands, then you can laser-focus your time and marketing dollars on this smaller audience of people rather than sprinkling these assets on a much larger population, the vast majority of whom are *not* in the market for your services right now.

This is called two-step marketing. Step one is the ad or marketing that you did to capture prospects' attention and get them to indicate their interest (and provide you with their contact information). Step two is the information you provide, which establishes you as an expert, builds trust with them, and presells them on doing business with you.

Wouldn't it be great to arrive at a prospect's home for a meeting and be in this position? You are no longer viewed as a salesman but welcomed into their home as an advisor. That, my friend, is where you want to be.

You can take this to an even higher level by making your consumer education piece even more closely matched to your target market.

"Warning, Greenville Homeowners, the Twenty-Five Questions You Absolutely, Positively…"

"Spring Hill Homeowners Association Members, Don't Make These Mistakes…"

"Pittsburgh Symphony Members, Twenty-Seven Secrets to Planning Your Luxury Kitchen…"

How else can you use this concept?

Rather than a consumer information packet, you could offer a no-obligation free consultation. People are suspicious of free consultations—they know you really want to sell them something—so you may want to offer that as a "next step" in the packet you send with the consumer information.

You could offer a free seminar or partner with someone to put on a seminar. I recall when I was younger and living in Indiana, a mortgage company was offering a free seminar targeted to people looking to build new homes. A custom home builder gave part of the presentation, and he was great. I'm certain he got some strong prospects from that seminar.

A free webinar might also work. In order to make a webinar work, you almost certainly have to have e-mail addresses of your prospects. One thing you may not know is that you can record a webinar and replay it over and over as if it were actually being held live. That would free you from having to do a new webinar every time you want to have one.

A video on your website would almost certainly improve your response rates.

Just remember, you're not selling. You are educating members of your community about your specific type of contracting, what to look out for, how to get the end result that they want, and what the important considerations are in selecting a contractor.

It's key in offering any of these options to collect contact information from the people who are asking to receive, attend, or view whatever it is that you have prepared. That's one of the biggest mistakes businesses make, especially contractors.

You must remember: people want things created especially for *them*. And by providing them with information on a topic that they don't know a lot about but are getting ready to spend a pretty big chunk of cash on, you begin to separate yourself from your competitors and gain their trust.

By approaching this upside down from the way every other contractor is approaching it, you become their trusted advisor rather than someone just trying to sell them something.

CHAPTER 5

The Importance of Marketing Math

We have to spend just a few minutes on some mundane but critically important topics. No, I'm not going to take you back to eighth-grade algebra. (My son is in eighth grade as I write this book, and I find that I'm having to repeat the grade myself.)

This math is much more straightforward…and unlike quadratic equations, you'll actually be able to use it!

Of all the chapters in this book, this is the one that you are most tempted to overlook, to put aside and say to yourself, "I don't really need to do this part…" I know this because of the work my partner and I have done with hundreds and hundreds of contractors.

Do me a favor. Just read the chapter and then you can decide whether it'll be useful to you or not. That's not asking too much, is it?

The first thing we're going to do is figure out your "lifetime customer value." Let's start by defining what I mean by lifetime customer value. It's the total combined profit you make over the lifetime of an average customer, including all repeat sales, referrals, impact of testimonials, and references they provide for you.

Let me give you an example.

Let's say that you're a home-remodeling contractor, and you are hired to do a bathroom remodel that generates $12,000 in revenue. The same customer hires you a few years later to finish their basement, which brings in $20,000. Then they hire you again a few years later to bump out their family room and add on a sunroom and a deck. Another $120,000.

Now let's figure out how much of that is profit to you. Let's say your net profit is 15 percent, so you made $22,800 in profit on that client. That's pretty good.

But wait...there's more.

Over the years, this customer referred you to a neighbor and to her sister, and these jobs totaled $60,000 in revenue. You calculate that the referrals generated profit in the amount of $9,000.

The customer also gave you a testimonial for the terrific job you did, and you used the testimonial in your marketing. You calculate the value of the testimonial at $500.

Finally, they agreed to be a reference for you, and they provided five positive references to prospective clients that called them. You calculate that each reference was worth $500, for a total value of $2,500.

This customer has been worth $215,000 in "value" to you and generated $34,800 in profit for you.

For certain contractors, the math will have an additional calculation. For example, if you're a pool and spa contractor and you also do pool maintenance, or a landscaping contractor and you also do landscape maintenance, then the numbers would look a bit different. You would calculate the value of the ongoing stream of revenue from these customers as well as the revenue from the initial installation.

Knowing these numbers has a huge impact on how you treat your prospects. Most contractors think the marketing stops when the phone rings.

They switch immediately into selling mode. Wrong! Remember, marketing is *everything you do to generate and keep customers for your business.*

Are prospects customers? Not yet. So your marketing needs to continue until they become a customer—and even after they become a customer so that they become a repeat customer and then a referral machine.

How Much Should You Spend to Attract a New Customer?

So, the question is, how much are you willing to spend to get this customer?

Your answer should be "a lot."

You see, when you take the strategies I outlined in the last chapter to narrow the number of people that you're focusing your marketing on, and combine them with your understanding of lifetime customer value, you can see how powerful that formula is.

Why couldn't you spend $150, or $200, or $250 on a "wow package" to send to the prospect that requested your consumer information? Why wouldn't you?

Your goal is to arrange your marketing system so that you can spend ten times, or twenty times, more than your competitors are willing to spend to woo your prescreened prospects. You're not necessarily spending that much more overall, but you are targeting your spending on people who have put their hands up and indicated that they are good prospects for you.

Can you see how powerful that is?

So, that video you've been thinking you should make to show prospects why and how you are different from your competition? Do it. Yes, it may cost you $10,000 or more to have it done right, but it's going to be worth every penny.

How about getting a professional photographer to take images of your projects, instead of you hastily shooting some pictures using your phone? Yup, do it. (This is critically important for your website, and if you intend to be listed on Houzz, which is image focused.)

How about putting some other stuff in the package that you send to clients…some interesting or fun food? The only excuse you need to have for including it can be that these huge chocolate chip cookies are your absolute favorite things in the world, and you want them to enjoy them while they are reading over your material.

You could give them a spa package that you've worked out with a local day spa. Or an evening of romance that includes a limo ride and dinner at a romantic restaurant. (You'll see where this idea comes from later on.)

Please understand this: the stuff in your wow box doesn't have to have anything to do with the job you are discussing with the prospect.

So your lifetime customer value, or LCV, is extremely important, and you need to spend some time to get a handle on this number. One quick and easy way to get a ballpark LCV is to take the number of jobs you did in the last two or three years, and divide your gross revenue by this number. Apply your net profit percentage to the figure, and there you are. This is your LCV.

So here's the equation:

$$\text{\# of jobs} \div \text{gross revenue} \times \text{net profit} = \text{LCV}$$

You may want to add 20 percent to this number to account for referrals and references.

How to Track Your Marketing Success

The next important item on your agenda is to implement a system so that you can capture the source of every single lead you get. You should devote another focus hour—or more—to this task.

What you want to know is the route prospects took to get to you. If they requested your consumer information from your website, you might give credit to your website for that lead. But what if they got to your website because you steered them there with a newspaper ad? Or what if they saw your yard sign and then went to your website? Or were referred by a family member but wanted to check out your website first?

Your script for a prospect call should include a little digging to find out how they first heard of you or came across your name.

The reason you need this information is because you are going to start tracking the effectiveness of each and every type of marketing that you do. If you're paying $750 a month for a Yellow Pages ad, and you determine that you got only one lead from it in a year, you may decide that it's not worth continuing. If you got four leads a month from that ad, and three of them became clients, then you'd likely want to continue it, depending on your LCV.

You'll want to calculate your cost per lead and your cost per sale from different marketing strategies.

In my Yellow Pages example, the cost per lead is $187.50, which we arrive at by dividing the cost of the ad, $750, by the number of leads generated, four.

The cost per sale is $250. We calculate this number by dividing the cost of the ad, again $750, by the number of sales made, three. That's pretty straightforward, isn't it?

By the way, a cost per sale of $250 is extraordinarily low, but we'll be talking about that some more in later chapters.

Let's say that you run an ad in a high-end area publication, which also costs you $750 per month, and the ad generates only one customer every month. So the cost per sale is $750. You might determine that the Yellow Pages is working better for you since it's delivering customers at a cost per sale of only $250.

But wait…let's take a closer look.

What if the average size of the job from the high-end publication is four times the average job from customers that came from the Yellow Pages? Well, that's important information. We all want to have fewer jobs that pay more, don't we? Maybe your decision then is to increase your spending with the high-end publication, buy a bigger ad, and try to get a better response.

So you can see how crucial it is to, first of all, understand your LCV, and then to track the different types of marketing that you do to determine which ones are performing and which ones are delivering the type of clients that are most profitable for you.

Okay, this ends our math lesson. I'm going to come back to these concepts in subsequent chapters, so it's important that you have a grasp on what they mean.

Realists versus Dreamers

Legendary British ad man, copywriter, and marketing consultant Drayton Bird, whom I had the privilege of meeting, says, "There are realists and there are dreamers…You've seen the dreamers, with their heads in the clouds. Realists know more and apply their knowledge."

In the contracting business, especially, we need to be realists in order to survive. We're all competing for the limited number of projects out there, and none of them wants to spend a dime more than they have to. In order to prosper rather than just survive, you need to know more *and* apply your knowledge.

Ignoring this chapter is dangerous. Understanding where your best clients come from—and especially understanding how much every client means to you—is essential information to a realist. How can you possibly determine the amount that you can spend to attract a client if you don't know your LCV? You can't. At best you're guessing.

The information in these pages will help you. Begin to apply the new knowledge that I've given you here. I think you'll agree that none of what I've talked about here is all that difficult.

CHAPTER 6

The Simple Way to Develop Your Marketing Game Plan

Alexander Graham Bell once said, "Before anything else, preparation is the key to success."

I have a confession to make. Paperwork, bookkeeping, and planning are not really my strongest attributes. I'm like a lot of entrepreneurs—just give me something to do, and I'll get it done. And then some. Ready, fire, aim is how I work.

For years I did just fine without doing much planning. I would begin each day with a pretty good idea of what needed to be accomplished, and I would get most of it done. Business was coming in, clients were generally happy, the business was profitable, and I was making a good income. I didn't see a problem.

Of course, I really didn't have a good handle on where my business was coming from, which marketing strategies were working and which were not, or how and why I was losing clients. I had no idea what my lifetime customer value was. I spent a lot of time working but no time doing strategic work.

I was working upside down…and I suspect you are too.

Looking back now, I can see that, had I created a marketing plan, I could have focused my marketing dollars much more wisely. I would have generated much more revenue and profit in my business without doing any more work, and my income would probably have been doubled.

I wish I had those dollars.

Now, don't confuse a business plan with a marketing plan. A business plan is a document that's oftentimes filled with data that your bank wants. It might include some "market data," but that's really fluff.

Some years ago, an acquaintance of mine asked me to look at his business plan. He wanted to quit his computer-programming job, buy a big sailboat, and start a business in Burlington, Vermont, taking tourists on sailboat rides on Lake Champlain. His plan was to offer gourmet dinner cruises, candlelight wine-tasting cruises, and so forth.

Not a bad idea for a business…at least it didn't *seem* to be a bad idea.

He'd done some market research, and based on the numbers the bank wanted to see, it looked like the business might just work. In fact, he'd gotten approval for his business loan from the bank.

But I wanted to ask him a couple of other questions, like what other options existed in Burlington that offered a similar experience, what other activities were there for tourists, and how many tourists—and what type of tourists—visited Burlington each year.

These questions had little to do with the "numbers" but a lot to do with marketing, especially finding a hungry market.

Well, it turned out that Burlington tended to draw a lot of families, which are generally not going to be interested in a romantic dinner cruise. There were lots of other options in or near Burlington for families, including the Vermont Teddy Bear Company factory and Ben & Jerry's. Wealthy people tended not to vacation in Burlington. In fact, even today, if you research lakefront homes in and around Burlington, you'll see that they are surprisingly affordable.

On my advice, he called the captain of the one ship that was operating cruises out of Burlington, and the guy was kind enough to tell him that they were getting ready to shut down…not enough people wanted to go on their lake cruises.

And the bank had offered my guy financing!

So, again, a business plan is not a marketing plan.

A marketing plan is, very simply, a road map that you outline for yourself based on your decisions about

1. how you want to do business,
2. what marketing strategies and messages you are going to use to attract customers to your business that you want to attract, and
3. how you will keep customers engaged and maximize your revenue from them.

Let's take a closer look at these points.

Decide How You Want to Do Business

I know this may come as a shock to you, but as the owner of your business, you get to decide how you want to do business.

Not only that but you also get to decide what you want to do and what you don't want to do.

This is upside-down thinking at an advanced level. Make your business compatible with the lifestyle you want—not the other way around.

A story…I'm involved in the Boy Scout troop that my son belongs to. I'm the guy who goes on all the campouts because there are never enough adults who want to hang around with a bunch of unruly teenagers; sleep in tents on the cold, hard ground; and eat food prepared by the scouts in pots that aren't exactly sparkling clean.

I'm also the guy who pulls the trailer because nobody else is comfortable doing it. (I worked on an apple farm in college, and every tractor had a trailer of one kind or another behind it. You learn real quick when you have to back a tractor up between rows of fragile trees with a trailer in tow, and the skill never leaves you.)

As I said earlier, paperwork is not my forte. But paperwork is part of the deal with the Boy Scouts. Reservations have to be made, logistics coordinated, plans filed with the council, and so on. Not my thing…and yet I was doing it.

Then, one day, Phil came into the picture. Phil's son is also in the troop, and Phil is a planner. He *loves* paperwork. Doesn't like to go on campouts, but he will happily organize the food, drivers, reservations, and insurance and medical forms; file the necessary permits; get everyone directions; and just make it happen.

Phil took all the stuff I hated and left me with the stuff I enjoy. (Yes, I admit I like sleeping in my tent and eating grub that the scouts have cooked.)

Here's the point: you can do the same in your business. There are people out there who love to do the things that you hate to do. And you can hire them. Full-time, part-time, on-site, virtual, temporary…all are options for you.

Believe me, I resisted hiring my first employee for way too long. It was only after a friend of mine told me his wife, Kristin, was looking for work ten hours a week that I finally decided to take the plunge. Kristin was amazing. She could do thirty hours of work in ten hours. My income almost doubled immediately after I hired her. And, like Phil, she was good at everything I was lousy at.

So, do you want to take every afternoon off of work, as I did for nine years, to spend with your kids after school? You can.

Instead of running your company, do you prefer to keep swinging your hammer, or working your shovel, or turning your wrench, or whatever? You can. Have you ever considered hiring someone else to be the chief operating officer of your company? You can do that, you know.

I gave my very own brother this advice. He's a plumber and doesn't want to run his company, deal with payroll, do the bookkeeping, mess with the computers, and all that. He wants to be on the truck. You *can* make it happen.

Do you finally want to take that two-week vacation that your wife has wanted to take for so long, and you've never done it because you can't get away for two weeks in a row? I'm telling you, you *can*.

This topic could fill a whole book by itself, so I'm not going to dwell on it. But look at every aspect of your business, think about how you could either delegate it or get rid of it, and then simply do it. Arrange your business to suit your lifestyle…not the other way around.

Decide on Your Marketing Strategies

We talked about selecting your target market earlier, and we said that selection of your marketing strategies has to flow from that decision. Clearly, you're not going to place windshield flyers on cars in the mall parking lot if you're looking for clients that are going to spend $50,000 to $100,000 or more on their landscaping, a new pool, or an addition.

What I'm talking about here is *planning* your marketing strategies. And the best tool I know of to do that is a marketing calendar.

A marketing calendar is really pretty simple. Go to the office-supply store, and buy a large calendar that you hang on the wall—the one that lets you write on it, then erase. I've found this to be the best for this purpose.

What you're going to do is to plan out your marketing on this calendar for the whole year.

Let's say that you plan to run a newspaper ad. First, you need to figure out when the newspaper needs your artwork in order to get the ad into the paper when you want it to run. From there you'll work backwards to determine

1. when you need to figure out what size ad you'll be running, usually dictated by your budget for the ad;
2. when you need to decide upon your offer;
3. when you need to get the ad to your graphic-design person;
4. when you need it back so that you have time to review it before it gets sent to the newspaper; and
5. when you will review it with your staff and employees.

All of these dates will go on your marketing calendar.

What about the strategies you'll use to keep your customers engaged and spending money with you?

Same thing.

Let's say you plan to send a monthly print newsletter to your customers. You first would target a date that you want the newsletter to go out. Let's say you want to mail it on the fifteenth of the month.

Well, it needs to be printed, labeled, and postage applied, so you need to allow a few days for that to happen. That means it needs to be written by the thirteenth of the month.

And you know it takes you at least a week to write the newsletter. So you need to put several items on your marketing calendar:

1. On the sixth of the month, you will start writing the newsletter.
2. Starting on the thirteenth, the newsletter will be printed, labeled, and stamped. (Staff has to make sure that postage is in the meter or stamps are purchased.)
3. Newsletter is mailed on the fifteenth.

You do this for each marketing strategy that you undertake. If you run a Yellow Pages ad, then you need to put the date that the ad is due on the calendar and a date sometime earlier to work on your ad.

One of the real benefits of using this technique is that you will no longer be tempted to engage in "random acts of marketing."

Random acts of marketing happen when a sales rep walks in the door and pitches you on advertising somewhere you hadn't ever considered, but makes a compelling argument, and you decide to do it.

Or the Yellow Pages rep comes in with a presentation to get you to increase the size of your ad or to add color, and you do it. Or someone mocks up a mobile website for you and sends it to you saying you absolutely *must* do this right away.

I think we're all guilty of falling for this at one time or another.

Well, with your marketing all planned out on your calendar, you are no longer under pressure to accept these offers on the spot. You'll be confident that you have your marketing well planned, and you can politely let ad reps know that they may leave their information with you. You'll consider them when you are planning your marketing for next year.

I don't want you to spend a lot of time right now developing your marketing calendar. In section III, Backwards Marketing, we'll look at a number of outstanding strategies for you to bring in new customers and keep your current customers engaged. I have a feeling that once you have finished reading this book, you'll abandon some of the tactics you're using now and start using some new ones.

To build a successful and highly profitable contracting business is going to require more than one or two methods for generating new clients. In fact, too many contractors make the mistake of relying on a very small number of marketing methods to generate all of their prospects and clients.

It can be a fatal error. One day the phone will stop ringing, and you might run out of money before you can figure out how to get it ringing again.

Most highly successful contracting businesses are built by using a number of proven, reliable marketing strategies to consistently generate new prospects and clients like clockwork. You can say good-bye to the usual "feast or famine" syndrome that so many contractors live with...One month you've got more work than you can handle; the next month you can't keep your guys busy.

By diversifying your marketing, if one method stops working, it's just a small dip, not a catastrophic event. Then we start testing other strategies to see what we're going to do to replace the one that stopped working.

The goal is to determine which methods, strategies, and processes will deliver the most desirable clients for you and for your business, which in turn will allow you to structure your business to support the lifestyle you desire.

Does that sound good?

I have a whole chapter dedicated to engaging your customers, so let's talk about that when we get there.

Now, let's go on to section II and talk about inside-out marketing.

SECTION II
Inside-Out Marketing

CHAPTER 7

Make Your Business *Fun*... and *Have* Fun

In the next few chapters, we're going to talk about "inside-out marketing."

What I mean by inside-out marketing is that you're going to let the outside world have a peek inside your business. This is a very powerful strategy in today's world.

In fact, a new term has become popular recently, which is "reality marketing." Reality marketing is just what I said...namely, showing people the inside reality of your company and letting them know that you care about them.

Before we jump into some of the specific methods to move your revenue and profits upward, I want to talk about making your business fun.

To me, it's vital that you not only make the business fun for your customers but also for yourself.

Here's something to think about. Surveys, studies, and research consistently reaffirm that 85 percent of your success depends on attitudinal factors, and only 15 percent on aptitude.

Yet almost everyone in business takes the opposite approach. They put 85 percent of the emphasis on aptitude—meaning their skill and knowledge—and only 15 percent on attitude. I'm going to suggest that you turn this around.

I'll talk first about how to make your business fun for you, then how to make it fun for your customers.

I can't tell you the number of contractors I speak to who complain that they hate their businesses.

"Hate" is a very strong word, but that's the term they use.

When we dig a little deeper, though, I almost always find that they're actually *bored* with their businesses. And who among us doesn't *hate* to be bored?

So they think they hate their businesses, but they're really in a rut of boredom. They dread going to work every day, they're rude to their employees, and they walk around with their heads hanging down wondering how they ended up in this mess.

They're distracted and less productive. Boredom is depleting. It empties the soul and crushes passion.

And it shows to prospects and customers. Employees don't treat the customers well because they don't get treated well by the boss. And, if the business owner thinks his disgust with the business can be hidden from the customers, then he's fooling himself.

I've come to the conclusion that entrepreneurial business owners get bored because they are fundamentally different from the rest of the population. You see, most people are wired for security. They want secure jobs, and they want to know that their paychecks are going to be there at regular intervals. They want reliable cars, solid relationships, and food on the table.

Entrepreneurs, though, are wired for challenge, for excitement, for risk. And once they have built a successful company, the challenge is no longer there for them. The excitement is lost, and boredom sets in.

The best advice that I can give you to pull yourself out of the rut of boredom is to...*change your role in your company.*

I recommend you do this even if you're not bored with your company. The truth is that your company needs you—or someone—to take command of the business.

Now, if you have a small operation, it might be impossible for you to lay down your tools and manage your company 100 percent of the time. That's okay. You still need to block out time to focus on moving the company forward.

And that's where you will be challenged...and start having fun again.

I have several suggestions to get you started. Here's a short story to make my point...

Like a lot of kids, I started playing a musical instrument in fifth grade. My instrument was trombone. I was not exactly a prodigy on the trombone, but I stuck with it through middle school and into high school.

For some reason, the summer between ninth and tenth grade, I suddenly got interested in improving my playing. I picked up that trombone every single day and practiced for an hour or two. And, lo and behold, in eight or ten short weeks, I went from being a middling player to being one of the best in my school.

Suddenly I was being asked to play in the jazz band, to join the "upper" band, and to play in the pit orchestra for the drama group. It changed everything for me. Most of my friends were in the band, and we did everything together.

Later, when I spent a year of college in Germany, I was able to join a local band there. It made the experience of being abroad so much richer for me since I was traveling all around the country, taking part in festivals and celebrations, and drinking with my band buddies, while all the other abroad students were hanging around with each other.

The point of my story is that spending even a small amount of time on a consistent basis focused on a specific objective will yield remarkable results.

The Power Hour

So, first, I want to recommend that you schedule a one-hour period for yourself each and every week to focus on building your business. This is an absolute minimum amount of time. Better would be twice a week or even every day. Carve this time in stone. Don't let anything distract you from taking this crucial hour of focus to work on your business.

You're going to use this hour to concentrate on marketing your business. Specifically, you're going to concentrate on how you can bring in new clients, make more sales, and deepen your relationships with your prospects and customers. You're going to give yourself the title of "chief marketing officer" for your business.

Ask yourself, "What one thing can I do this week to make progress toward my goal of bringing in more customers?" After all, what is more important than new customers coming into your business?

Don't worry. There are lots of great strategies in the upcoming chapters that will make this job easy. I promise you won't be staring at the wall wondering what to do during your hour of focus. You'll have plenty to do.

Structure Your Business to Suit You

It's also important for you to decide *how* you want to do business. Whenever I talk to business owners and tell them that they can structure their businesses to suit their lifestyles, they tell me I'm crazy. Their businesses, their clients, and their employees would never stand for a business owner who isn't available 24/7, who doesn't respond instantly to a call or problem, and so forth.

Baloney. When I was running my employee-benefits business, my clients were constantly facing huge premiums increases on their health insurance plans, claims that were being denied by the insurance companies, billing errors, employees who didn't get enrolled, deadlines, and on and on.

Yet I was able to take off every afternoon—leaving my office at two thirty—during the time that my son was in preschool and grade school. That's every afternoon for nine years. And it was during this time that my business experienced the most dramatic growth. My revenues and profits, on average, at least doubled every year.

So I'm telling you that it *is* possible...and I wouldn't trade those afternoons spent with my son for anything in the world.

Every business owner I know of who has made these changes— taken time to focus on their business and structured their business to suit themselves—has found that it's enlivening...and very, very impactful on the bottom line. It's a new challenge that requires your most intense effort, and I think that's what makes it so satisfying to entrepreneurs and business owners.

We'll be coming back to this theme throughout the book.

Make It Fun for Your Customers

Now, the second part of this formula is that you have to make it fun for your customers.

You're going to accomplish this by entertaining your customers with interesting, humorous, and fascinating marketing that they will enjoy and look forward to getting from you.

And, if you follow my advice, you're going to have fun doing it. Let's look at just one example...

Let's say that you're going to send an e-mail or a letter out to your customers. Rather than just any old letter, though, this one is going to come from your staff rather than from you. And, instead of being a "typical" message that talks about how great you are and what services you provide, the message starts with a picture of your office staff looking frazzled, and up to their ears in boxes of pasta, with limp spaghetti hanging from their heads.

The message is that you, the evil boss, told them that you wanted them to send this e-mail or letter out to all of the customers. But you got a delivery of a hundred boxes of pasta that day, which you're eating because you recently started on a high-carbohydrate diet. Every corner of the office is filled up with pasta of every imaginable shape and size, which you cook up at lunchtime for yourself in the office kitchen (of course, never sharing any with them).

There's hardly room to even move in the office much less get anything done. But, after struggling for hours, tripping over the boxes of pasta lying everywhere, and getting really mad at the computers and printers, they finally managed to get it done.

The message ends with "Well, after all that, here's why the *boss* wanted us to send you this e-mail..." And that's where you put your offer.

Now, let me ask you a question: Wouldn't you rather get an amusing e-mail like that than a bland, boring e-mail?

And do you think your customers will read the next message from you, or just delete it or toss it like they do every other e-mail or piece of junk mail?

And when they call in, don't you think they'll share a laugh with the staff about the pasta message that "they" wrote?

I like to call this sort of marketing "sensational" marketing because it's both appealing and it works really well. Others call it "outrageous." You might call it unconventional, abnormal, extraordinary, uncommon, or even wacky. Call it whatever you want; the bottom line is that it's different than what everyone else is doing, and it gets attention because it's different.

You see, I believe that ordinary marketing gets ordinary results. And if what you want is an ordinary result, then you should do the same thing everyone else in your industry is doing.

But dreaming up ideas to do sensational marketing is fun. And it's fun for your target audience to get marketing messages that are unusual, or delivered in unconventional ways.

As we progress through this book, we'll look at a lot of ways for you to be original in your marketing. Rather than reject these ideas, I encourage you to embrace them.

Oliver Wendell Holmes said, "The greatest thing in this world is not so much where we are, but the direction in which we are moving."

He couldn't be more right...at least as far as entrepreneurs are concerned. I'm guessing that you went into business because you wanted freedom, you didn't want somebody else putting limits on you, and you wanted to create a lifestyle that you dreamed about.

I want *you* to move in that direction.

Challenge yourself to have more fun in your business. If you like your business, you'll want to spend more time with it. You'll be happier. And you'll make more money when you're happier in what you're doing.

So, make your business fun both for yourself and for your customers, and then use inside-out marketing to show the world.

CHAPTER 8

Turn Your Customers into Raving Fans

You most likely have a business that you just love to buy from. It might be a local coffee shop or restaurant that you visit often, a hardware store, your veterinarian, a clothing store, a car parts store, or an antique shop. From a business perspective, it might be a lumberyard or a supply house.

Do you have a business or a store in mind that you feel this way about? For me it's my local hardware store. It's an old-time store that still carries everything you could need or want. I probably love it because I worked in a similar hardware store throughout my high school and college years.

Something makes it pleasant for you to visit these businesses, and you enjoy going. And when you go, you probably buy something.

You might not even be able to put your finger on exactly what it is that you like about going there. And if anyone asks you where to buy the product that this store or business sells, there's absolutely no doubt that you would recommend this business and no other.

You are a raving fan.

In this chapter, I'm going to spend a little time talking about why it's important to have raving fans and how to turn your customers into raving fans.

It's no secret that the lifeblood of every contracting business is new leads. And the very best leads are those that are referred to you. Referrals tend to be much less price-motivated, are generally easier to close, and are more likely to listen to your advice and take your recommendations.

Word-of-mouth marketing has always been important in the contracting world but is far *more* important now than ever before. With online directories like Yelp and Google+ Local, services like Angie's List, HomeAdvisor, Houzz, Porch—and the fact that dissatisfied customers can e-mail hundreds and hundreds of people with a few keystrokes—it's essential that you have supporters and not critics.

And people are much more sensitive to negative comments than to positive comments. My wife, when she looks for a hotel or restaurant on a site like TripAdvisor, has her own formula she uses—if the number of comments in the bottom two categories is more than 10 percent of the number in the top two, she rules the hotel or restaurant out.

So if your business has a hundred good and great reviews, and fifteen so-so or bad reviews, she wouldn't hire you. And I don't think she's alone in the way she makes her decisions. It's a brutal world out there.

And whether you think she's unreasonable doesn't matter…She gets to use whatever criteria she wants to make her decisions.

So we all agree that having raving fans is good.

Are You "Just Okay"?

I'm going to move it up a notch and tell you that, in today's relentlessly competitive environment, it's critical to your survival that you cultivate raving fans.

Recently, I decided that I'd lived long enough without the luxury of a housekeeper, and I wanted to hire one to clean my home once a week. I called a neighbor of mine and asked him how he liked his housekeepers.

"Well," he said, "they're okay...just okay."

Hmmm.

I called another neighbor and asked the same question.

"They're great. Best we've ever had. They're not the cheapest, but I wouldn't hesitate to recommend them."

Clearly, I'm going to see if I can hire the second one. And I'm going to pay more than the going rate for a housekeeping service. I want to be a raving fan, you see. I don't want to be aggravated every Thursday when I get home and see all the little things they forgot to do or didn't clean to my satisfaction.

If your customers are telling people that you're "okay," you've got a big problem.

Let's talk about how to get them to say, "They're great! I wouldn't hesitate to recommend them."

Start with a Customer Focus

Now, before I dive into this topic, I want to say that doing top-notch work is a basic requirement. In other words, if you follow all the advice in this chapter, but the quality of the work that you do is lacking, then you'll be wasting your time.

So the very first requirement if you want glowing referrals is to do exceptional work, and treat your customers like royalty. You want to be so professional and do such high-quality work that the customer is blown away.

In order to become the kind of contractor that customers will passionately endorse, you have to care about them. You have to start with a customer focus. You'll need to look at the impact that your work is having on them, on their lives, and on their families. Recognize that it's stressful and disruptive to have a contractor doing a project in your home or on your property.

Notice how this ties in with the earlier messages about putting yourself into the customer's shoes. It's very much the same thing.

To the greatest extent possible, you want to make it easy and convenient for people to do business with you.

Get Control of Your Phone

Let's start at the beginning. The ultimate purpose of your marketing is to get the phone to ring, right? It's the entry point for most prospects, and the method most of your customers will use to communicate with you. And nothing happens without a customer…no sale…no money.

What happens when someone calls *your* company? Is the call answered? Every time?

Is the caller greeted in a professional, enthusiastic way? Every time?

Does the person answering the phone have a script that is followed? Every time?

Look, I know the answer to these questions for the vast majority of contractors. The phone does *not* get answered. A call is viewed by you and your employees as an intrusion…an inconvenience. And there is no script.

The number one complaint, by far, that consumers have about contractors is that they don't answer the phone. The second is that they don't return calls.

How can you show buyers the inside of your company if they can't even get you on the phone?

You *must* get the phone under control if you want to have raving fans.

Let me tell you a short story…okay, maybe not so short. But important.

My brother is a plumber, and a darned good one. When he does an installation, everything is perfectly plumb and square. He takes extra time and care to make sure that his work is top-notch, even if it eventually ends up inside a wall. Some people call him "old school" because he refuses to cut corners and insists on doing the job right…every time.

In school, my brother wasn't a poor student by any means, but school wasn't giving him what he wanted. You see, he has a different kind of intelligence than schools tend to measure, and he decided to leave college after his first year to pursue a career in the trades. The kind of intelligence he has makes him an artist with his hands. I suspect you are a lot like him.

Now, I love my brother. He's rough and gruff, but his heart is huge, and he'd do just about anything for his family and friends. If there's one person in this world I know I can count on in a pinch, it's him. He's godfather to my son, and the tenderness he shows to my son is incredible.

Some years ago I started a tradition of arranging a fishing trip once a year with my brothers—I have two of them, an older one and a younger one. I wanted to make sure that I got a chance to spend a little time with them at least once a year. It's a great trip, and we all look forward to it.

The routine is that I pick up my older brother—the plumber—at his house, and we drive three hours to Rhode Island. My younger brother, who lives close to Boston, meets us there. We have some beers, shoot the breeze, have a nice dinner, and then hit the sack. The next day we go fishing and usually pull a good supply of stripers and bluefish out of Block Island Sound. Then we load up the coolers and head back home.

During the long car rides, my brother will often get calls on his mobile phone. He'll look at the screen to see if he recognizes the number. He usually lets it go to voice mail; then he immediately listens to the message. Most often it's someone who needs his services and wants to hire him. Yet he doesn't return the call.

I have never understood why he doesn't just answer the call, and I've never asked him. I guess I feel like it's none of my business.

But I promise you, his customers and potential customers are complaining that they can't get a hold of him and that he doesn't return his calls.

So I started my research by asking myself, what could it be about the personality traits of people in the trades that makes the phone so difficult for them to deal with?

What I discovered is very interesting. I wrote a separate article about my research, which you can find at www.bernieheer.com. The main points are

- everyone is intelligent in one or more ways;
- most contractors are gifted in ways that our schools and our society don't value as highly as they should, and these people are sometimes falsely labeled as unintelligent; and
- the specific personality makeup of the type of people who enter the trades makes answering the phone very difficult if not almost impossible.

I encourage you to read my full article if this topic interests you. Again, you can find it at www.bernieheer.com.

The simple solution is to hire people who are gifted in ways that you are not. There are personality types out there who actually look forward to phone calls, and who love talking to people and doing your planning and scheduling. If you don't have an office staff, then you should hire an answering service. I have found their rates to be surprisingly affordable.

Let's get back to handling the phone call itself.

The first fifteen seconds of the call are critical. The way the phone should be answered follows this formula: greeting, business name, your name, if possible a value statement, and a request for the caller's name. So it sounds something like this: "Thank you for calling Revolutionary Building; this is Lisa. We believe that everyone deserves a nicer, more comfortable home. May I ask your name?"

Now, other than sales calls, there are generally going to be only three reasons that people are calling:

- They're interested in your services.
- They have a question or problem.
- They're price shoppers.

You need to write a script for the receptionist to follow for each type of caller.

Since this is such a big problem in the contracting industry, I want to take just a minute longer to hammer home why fixing the phone is so crucial.

Let's say that you've determined that every lead is worth $1,000. (I'm guessing this number is very low for your business, but let's stick with it for this example.)

If you fail to convert one call a day, that's $1,000 lost. In a week, that's $5,000 lost. In a month, you've lost $20,000. In a year, $240,000 dollars lost simply because you failed to get your phone process working.

What if it's two calls a day?

So, right off the bat, you've lost incredible amounts of money by ignoring the problem of the phone. Maybe worse…you won't have raving fans. If you're not showing your clients the love, they aren't going to love you back.

Please, let's put a dent in the reputation that contractors have for not answering or returning their calls. It'll have a bigger impact than you can imagine.

Enough about the phone...

Hire Passionate Employees

If your employees aren't excited and enthusiastic about the services you provide, then they should probably be working somewhere else.

I once had an employee who was a wonderful person. I'd heard that I should "hire personality," so I did. Before working for me, she worked in a very high-end shoe store, selling women's shoes for thousands of dollars a pair. She had a terrific personality, and I figured she'd be great.

But her passion was for fashion and design. She was a terrific person but not so terrific for my business.

Passionate people care about customers. They want customers to be happy. When hiring employees, don't give too much weight to whether they "know" your business. Give more weight to whether they are empathetic and care about people.

Make It Hassle-Free for Customers to Do Business with You

Some businesses make it hard to be a customer.

When I moved my office a few years ago, the auto-repair shop I was using was no longer convenient, so I started using one close to my new office.

What I quickly discovered is that they open late and close early. I've never known of an auto shop that opens at nine and closes at four thirty, but this one does. Although I'm all for structuring your business to suit your lifestyle, I think an auto-repair shop owner also needs to recognize that the doors need to be open when customers can be there.

Anyway, I used them twice and then decided it was too much hassle for me to work around their schedule, and I started using a different shop.

I want you to make it completely hassle-free to be a customer.

Again, put yourself in your customers' shoes and ask yourself, "What can I do to make it easier for people to be my customers?" You may even want to ask some of your customers that question.

My neighbor recently moved out of the area, and the moving company e-mailed him pictures of the guys who would be packing up his belongings, along with a one-paragraph bio about each of them. My neighbor really appreciated that they did this because it made his wife feel a lot more comfortable.

The mover obviously put himself into the customer's shoes and figured out a way to relieve a concern that people have about strangers handling their possessions. Very smart. You could copy that idea.

As a start, consider these areas of your company:

1. Your hours of operation
2. The methods of payment you accept
3. Do you offer financing?
4. Is it easy for people to find you?
5. Make it a company policy to be on time for appointments.
6. Is there a long wait time to get an appointment?
7. Is it easy for your customers to get a problem resolved?
8. Are your vehicles clean and neat looking?
9. Do your employees wear uniforms or company shirts?
10. Do you safeguard customers' homes, property, and possessions during a project?
11. Do you make it easy for friends, family, or customers to refer others?

Don't underestimate the value of making it easy and convenient to be a customer. The easier you make it, the more raving fans you'll have.

Make It *Fun* to Be a Customer

In chapter 7, I talked about how to make your marketing fun and different from what your competitors are doing. That's one piece of the puzzle, but I want to talk about some more strategies to make it fun to be your customer.

I'd like you to think about ways that you can add a fun factor to everything you do.

For instance, instead of just sending a thank-you letter (I hope you're sending thank-you letters), include a five-dollar gift certificate to your favorite coffee shop and write in the thank-you letter that this is your favorite place for a hot cup of joe in the morning. And say, "Be sure to tell Pete, the owner, that I said hi."

What about sending all of your customers a postcard from your vacation? You can even have them all printed up and addressed ahead of time so that when you get to your vacation spot, you just drop them in a mailbox.

If you see an article in the newspaper about one of your customers, cut the article out and send it to them with a note. For instance, if their child was in a play or won an award at school, you would send the newspaper article with a nice note simply saying, "I saw you were in the news...congratulations!"

There's a plumber in Pennsylvania named Larry Rivellese who calls himself "the Singing Plumber." When he comes to your house, he greets you with an operetta. Fun!

You don't have to sing opera to have fun. Why not offer a lottery ticket if a customer tells you a good joke you haven't heard before? Of course, everyone gets the lottery ticket, whether the joke is any good or not...and whether you've heard it before or not. Make it two lottery tickets if their child tells you a joke (and be sure to laugh really hard).

Have a customer appreciation event. I've seen contractors do lots of different things: a pizza party, burgers and hot dogs at their shop, or cider and donuts in the fall. You could rent a theater and show a classic film, inviting all of your customers and their friends. Afterward, have a table set up with desserts that they can grab. One of the best—and easiest—is to buy every customer that shows up an ice-cream cone at a local ice-cream shop on a summer evening. It doesn't have to be complicated.

Send your customers a birthday card. Or an anniversary card. If you failed to capture this information from them, send them a "Happy Birthday to Your Kitchen" card on the anniversary of the completion of their kitchen.

Controlling Damage

Even the most skilled contractor makes mistakes from time to time. Sometimes it's not even your fault...It could be that an appliance or a piece of equipment that you installed is defective.

How you handle these situations will determine whether your customers become raving fans or not.

One of the most powerful actions we can offer to customers—especially those who aren't 100 percent happy with us right now—is an apology.

Now, the typical apology will go something like this: "I'm so sorry you're having trouble with the dishwasher we installed last week, Mrs. Jones, but you see, my technician was at his brother's bachelor party the night before, and he must've been cross-eyed when he installed it."

Or, "It's a manufacturing defect…"

Or, "[Some other reason…]"

Guess what, the customer doesn't care what the reason is that the job didn't come out right. She just wants it fixed—and soon.

I recommend what Jerry Wilson, author of *Word-of-Mouth Marketing*, calls the "naked apology." Don't try to justify why something went wrong. Not only do customers not care, it makes you seem shifty.

Instead, try this approach: "Mrs. Jones, I can see you're upset that the work we did for you didn't meet your expectations. I'm sorry. I'm coming to fix the problem right now. Is there anything else I can do for you to make this right?"

You'll be surprised. Most people just want their problem fixed and will be pleasantly surprised by your open, naked, unjustified apology.

Whether it was your error or not, failing to fix the problem will cost you far more in lost business than it will ever cost to fix the problem. And when you later tell Mrs. Jones that the dishwasher was defective from the manufacturer, she'll sing your praises for not charging her to pull it out and install the new one.

And one more thing—do yourself a favor, and send Mrs. Jones some movie tickets, a gift certificate to a local restaurant, or a book of car-wash coupons as a surprise once the problem is fixed. It'll be money well spent.

Another instance where you'll need to consider long-term consequences is when you've priced your estimate incorrectly or the customer misunderstood what was included in your proposal.

Let's say that you didn't include something in your proposal that the customer thought was included, an honest mistake on both sides. You'd like to get paid for the work, and the customer thinks it's already been paid for.

If you insist that the service wasn't included and show the customer where in the contract it is (or isn't), you'll most likely sour the whole relationship.

Now, if the disagreement is for a large sum of money, this approach may not work. But if it's for an amount that you can live with, you might say, "You know what, Mrs. Jones, this was an honest misunderstanding. I'm going to take care of this for you at no charge…but there's a catch."

Mrs. Jones says, "What's the catch?"

"The catch is, the next time someone you know is thinking about doing any building or remodeling work, you'll recommend me."

A slightly different approach would be: "Mrs. Jones, I'll make a deal with you."

"What's the deal?"

"I'll take care of this for you at no charge, but the next time you need any work done, you'll call me…or if you know someone who is thinking about doing any building or remodeling work, you'll recommend me."

It's surprising. Once people make that sort of agreement with you, assuming you've done a good job, they'll live up to their end of the bargain and call you or recommend you. And you'll end up making much more on those jobs than the amount you had to eat to make them happy.

Now, I'm not pretending that there aren't people out there who will try to take advantage of you and claim that they misunderstood your proposal just to get something out of you. We all know that happens way too often.

My advice is to give them the benefit of the doubt the first time—assuming it's not a big-cost item—but then put a stop to it if it happens again. That's when you take out your agreement and show them exactly where it states what they were paying for. If you give in more than once, they'll nickel-and-dime you to death *and* they'll post poor reviews on top of it.

This approach can also work well if you discover something relatively minor during a demolition phase that was unexpected. If you agree to do the extra work at no charge, you'll create a raving fan.

Make it easy and convenient to do business with you...Hire passionate, enthusiastic employees...Look at each situation from your customer's point of view...Make it fun to be a customer of yours...And know when to let the client win.

You'll have a whole flock of raving fans.

CHAPTER 9

Give Your Internet Marketing Superpowers

These days, if you don't have a website, you don't have a business.

A professional website is, today, like a business card was in years gone by. It's a basic necessity for a business.

I'm amazed at the number of contractors that still don't have a web presence. You'll never break through to the kind of income you should be making if you refuse to invest some money in a quality website.

Why is a website so important?

Well, first off, many people—myself included—never look at a Yellow Pages book anymore. I have a computer in my kitchen that's always on, and I use it to find information about pretty much everything. If I'm looking for a builder, that's where I'm going to search.

Also, the majority of people want to check you out before they call you. Even if they've gotten a strong recommendation from a family member or friend, they will want to go to your website to see what you're all about and whether you can solve their problem.

If they don't find your website—or your website is the same as everyone else's—then that's a big strike against you. They may eliminate you from consideration.

Now, it's also important to understand that you are not an Internet-based business. For most local businesses, a website is a tool that's an add-on to the core marketing strategies that will drive your customer acquisition. You need a web presence, but you don't need a complicated, expensive website.

You can get a fairly nice website designed and put up for $1,500 to $2,000. This isn't going to be a full-blown e-commerce website, but it will serve to establish an online presence for your business. And as you'll see in a moment, that may be all-you need.

Yes, you can get a website for much less than that by having your daughter or your niece or your neighbor's kid put something together for you using a free or very low-cost hosting platform, but it won't be very professional looking, and I don't suggest going this route.

If you want to build your website yourself, there are several organizations that have instructions and tools you can use. I have to warn you, though, it's going to take time. Probably a lot of time. And, as the billionaire investor Warren Buffett said when asked about the secret to his success, "Do what you know, and do it well."

In other words, better for you to build a house or remodel a kitchen, and leave the building of your website to someone qualified to do it.

I am not an expert on building websites. Nor am I an expert on search engine optimization (SEO), social media, or pay-per-click campaigns. I'm not going to address the technical aspects of any of these. Whole books have been written on each of these topics by people who are much more qualified than I am.

Marketing Considerations for Your Website

What I'm going to do is talk about what's important, which is for you to understand the *marketing considerations* so that you can properly direct the person or the vendor that's handling these different aspects of your Internet marketing strategy. These folks rarely understand marketing, so you're going to have to tell them what you want them to do.

Choosing and creating the design of your website is pivotal to its success, meaning its contribution to your bottom line. You want to design a site that's clean and simple, is attractive to potential customers, and keeps them engaged once they're there. Here are a couple of very basic rules for website design:

- People don't want to read a lot of text.
- They like pictures and graphics.
- They will read the captions under pictures and graphics.
- They don't like animated or flashy graphics littering a site.
- They don't like sites with dark backgrounds or text written in reverse color (light text on dark background).
- They enjoy sites that are direct and to the point.
- They enjoy finding exclusive offers.

In deciding what sort of information you'll have on your website, I suggest you ask yourself several questions.

Who will be coming to your website?

The answer to that question might seem obvious to you—prospective customers. And that'll be true for most contracting businesses.

But let's say that you've decided to focus on interior designers as a referral source. Well, that's going to change what you have on your website.

Instead of information of interest to the homeowner, you're going to have information that's interesting and helpful to interior designers.

What if you decide to focus on older homeowners who want to "age in place," and you are going to partner with physical therapists to refer their clients to you? Here again, you'll want to put information that's of interest to them, including trends and products that are new and will impact their clients.

In both of these instances, it probably makes sense for you to have two separate websites, one for the general public and another for the referral sources you want to work with.

What questions will visitors have?

This is a critically important consideration. Put yourself in your visitors' shoes—there's that recurring theme again—and imagine what questions they have that they're seeking answers to. Obviously you'll need to answer these questions on your website.

What do you want your visitors to do?

So few businesses ask themselves this question, which results in millions of websites that are nothing but online brochures.

There are all kinds of things you can offer your visitors to engage them and to enable you to gather their contact information. Here are some thoughts on what you might want your visitors to do:

1. Call your office to schedule a free consultation (difficult to do...).
2. Complete a web form to request your free consumer information. (We talked about this in chapter 4.)
3. Sign up to get a series of e-mails about important considerations in their decision to build or renovate a home.
4. Sign up to start getting your monthly newsletter sent to them.

5. Take a quiz about the impact of your services on the value of their home.
6. Take some other action or request other information from you.

You'll want to design your website so that visitors are steered toward taking the action that you want them to take. Usually that's going to be to call you or give you their contact information so that you can call them.

How will you get people to your website?

For most contractors, you'll include your website address in your ads and other marketing. You'll have it on your business card, on your stationery, and on any other marketing material you use.

But the foremost goal is to get people to your site who are searching on the Internet.

For example, if you're a building contractor in Springfield, Missouri, when someone searches the term "builder springfield mo" or a similar keyword, you want your website to come up very close to the top of the list that the search engine delivers.

There are a lot of factors that work together to make this happen—SEO, pay-per-click, directory listings, videos, average view time, and a lot more. The purpose of this chapter is not to get into those details, so I'm not going to focus on them. Again, entire books have been written on each of these topics, so it's really not possible to cover them in this book.

And I'll say again that I don't think it's wise for you to try to figure all of these things out. Better for you to spend your time doing what you do best, and let the folks who know what they're doing handle these tasks.

E-mail Marketing

How many e-mails do you get every day? I'm guessing too many.

How many of them get deleted without you reading them? I'm guessing most of them.

It's no secret that e-mail marketing is overused. People no longer open most of their e-mails. The big e-mail marketers survive on razor-thin response percentages, which is only possible because e-mail is close to free.

So, knowing this, is it worth doing e-mail marketing?

I gave you an example earlier about how to put fun into your e-mails. Here's another way to make it fun.

Some years ago, I was speaking to a highly successful marketer from Chicago who'd made his millions in the insurance and investment field. He confided in me that the single most successful marketing strategy he ever had was one that wasn't even intended to generate any sales.

You see, his passion is good food and wine. He decided, for fun, to write a weekly e-mail to all of his clients about a good bottle of wine he'd had, or a nice meal he'd enjoyed at a restaurant in the Chicago area, or a great food market he'd discovered where you could get interesting or unusual food items.

Well, his e-mail became very popular with his clients and friends. He would get e-mails back from people asking him to add their friends, neighbors, and family members to the e-mail list. It just grew and grew.

And guess what? Over time these former strangers got to know him personally through his food-and-wine e-mails. And when they needed some financial advice, they contacted him—even though he'd never written a single word in his e-mails about his financial-consulting practice.

My advice to you is to do exactly what this financial advisor did. Pick a topic that you're passionate about and write about it.

Whether you love the outdoors, are into dogs, like to grill, brew your own beer or wine, follow NASCAR, are a marathon runner, or enjoy any hobby or interest, write about it in your e-mail. You could even mix it up so that you have different topics you can pick from every week.

It's okay to put information about your specific trade from time to time. This shouldn't be the focus, but when important news or new product innovations are introduced, you can certainly let your e-mail list know about them.

Keep them short—around three hundred words—and don't be afraid to share a little bit about yourself. This is a slightly different twist on inside-out marketing. You're letting people see inside your personal life.

If you like, you can shoot a video from time to time and post it on YouTube. Then put a link to the video in your e-mail so that people can go and watch it.

In chapter 12, we'll talk about writing headlines. Writing the subject line for an e-mail is very much like writing a headline for an ad. You're going to write something compelling so that recipients will become interested and open your e-mails.

You may also decide to put your e-mails on your website. That's a good idea. When done this way, it's often called a blog. You can let people read all of your past messages and even give them a way to sign up to receive your e-mails directly.

The most critical thing you have to do is avoid being boring. That's the mistake most e-mail marketers make. They're boring, and all they want to do is sell.

Get this right, and people will forward your e-mails to others, and then those people will ask to be put on your e-mail list. That, of course, is what you're hoping for.

What About Social Media?

Don't be confused about what social media is and what it can do.

And don't confuse it with your website. Your website is where people can find your company information online, like a brochure in some ways. If built the right way, it will also capture visitors' information so that you can stay in touch with those that don't become customers and, hopefully, turn them into customers down the road.

Social media is usually not going to generate customers for you…at least not directly. It's more about having an ongoing conversation with people.

Think about a relationship you have with a longtime friend. You see your friend, and what do you do? You say, "Listen to what happened to me yesterday…" Or, "What'd you think of the game last night?" Or, "I saw a great movie over the weekend…"

That's exactly what you want to do on social media. You want to connect with people. You're not selling. Instead, you're sharing interesting information, maybe some photos, talking about something that happened to you, or even asking for input from your circle of connections.

In many ways, the thinking I outlined for your e-mail marketing translates directly to social media.

The names that are big in social media, at least right now, are Facebook, Twitter, LinkedIn, Pinterest, YouTube, and Instagram. These will most likely change over time.

Here's the most important thing to know about social media: people participate in these communities with no desire to buy anything.

That's very different from the people who land on your website. When people search the Internet for a contractor, they're looking for someone to hire.

Social media is closer to public relations than anything else. Businesses use PR to get their names and stories in the media. If you engage in social media, you will do so to be part of the community and to gain top-of-mind status with your target audience.

If there's one thing that social media can do for you, it's to be a referral platform. Along with the goals I mentioned above, you'd like to have people mention you if one of their connections asks for a referral to a good contractor. And the way social media platforms are set up, it's a simple matter of a click for someone to share your information with others.

For most contractors, social media will not be a major traffic source. But it will help you to discover things about your target market that you are not likely to learn any other way. And it will most likely bring you some customers that you may not have gotten otherwise.

Whether you want to admit it or not, Internet marketing is here to stay and is only going to grow in importance as time goes on. Disregarding it is only going to put you farther and farther behind your competitors.

CHAPTER 10

You Must Have a Bold Mind-Set

I'm a believer in the power of bold thinking and in having a mind-set of courage. In my experience, it's almost unheard of to find a successful business owner who doesn't have a strong tendency to think boldly.

Still, it's something we have to work on—to stretch ourselves, to exercise that muscle and build it up.

It's hard to do.

Thinking boldly may be the most critical single thing you do as a business owner and entrepreneur.

Very simply, without constant bold thinking, sales and profits dry up, businesses fail, and fortunes are lost.

In this chapter, I'm taking a little detour to outline seven "big ideas" to help you think more boldly in your business.

Ambition

"Ambition" has become a dirty word.

In generations past, a young man was praised for being ambitious, for wanting to improve his position in the world, and for wanting success and a comfortable life for his family.

Nowadays, when people hear that a young person is ambitious, they are likely to roll their eyes and scoff at him or her. There is a sense that, in order for one person to get ahead, another has to suffer.

Nothing could be further from the truth. Your success does not mean that someone else has to lose. Money is not a zero-sum game.

Ambition—to me—is:

- the belief in your ideas and their power,
- the self-belief that you can achieve your goals, and
- the overwhelming will to see them through.

Do those attributes sound bad to you?

Ambition is a good thing. Don't be afraid of your ambitions—embrace them. The world will be a better place.

Confidence

Earlier I wrote about the different types of intelligence and the fact that our schools and our society undervalue most types of intelligence.

Those of us who enter the trades tend to be strong in these undervalued intelligences, and that can lead to a serious lack of confidence.

Listen up!

You are an expert in your field. You have spent a great deal of time mastering skills most people cannot master, investing in tools and machinery, taking risks, and building a business.

You employ people, add to the economy, and are a contributing member of your community and our society.

Hold your head high!

No one outside of the industry knows what you know—not the customer, not their best friend, not their spouse or neighbor or cousin or mother-in-law. They *think* they know what you know—in fact, they think they know *better* than you—but they're clueless.

Don't let your customers, your family members, your competitors, or your industry dictate how you do business.

Now, don't confuse confidence with arrogance. Be sure of yourself without sneering or resorting to demeaning comments. Realize that others *don't know what they don't know*. You have to be patient with them.

You're a professional. You can behave like one. You don't need to prove your superiority, but always know that it's there.

Resourcefulness

Like ambition, resourcefulness is quickly becoming a rare trait.

I was on a flight just yesterday sitting in the very first seat on the plane, where I had a view into the galley area.

Something was wrong with the device that locks the coffeepot in place for takeoff and landing. Three flight attendants tried to pull the handle down and couldn't. One after another simply shrugged and walked off.

A fourth flight attendant tried as well. But, instead of leaving it, she looked closely at the mechanism, then got a butter knife from her stash and used it to pry apart whatever was stuck. The lock then worked perfectly.

Resourcefulness. Refusal to hear the words "no," "can't," or "impossible." A willingness to try to solve a problem instead of waiting for others.

In the face of change, too many business owners would rather wait for someone else to come to their rescue than to undertake bold action on their own.

It's a huge mistake.

Change is *always* coming. Be the first to embrace it, figure it out, adapt to it, and profit from it.

Quickness

Related to resourcefulness, quickness—or speed—is an essential quality for a business owner and is a sure sign of a boldness mind-set.

A sense of urgency, impatience, and decisiveness are the marks of the bold-thinking entrepreneur.

Most people feel that there is a logical sequence or an order in which things need to get done.

That's slow.

The bold thinker does them all at once. Simultaneously.

It requires courage, but the payoff can be huge.

Realism

Bold thinkers are realistic.

They recognize that others have strengths that they do not possess. They focus on the jobs that best suit their own strengths, and leave other jobs to other people.

By doing so, they are able to structure their businesses to suit themselves and their lifestyles.

You see, the bold-thinking contractor is not a slave to his business, always on the hamster wheel, never able to catch up on the mountain of work still to be done.

Instead, he has recognized that the business exists to feed his lifestyle choices. He carefully selects only those parts of the business that he enjoys, letting others attend to the tasks that he does not enjoy.

This is perhaps the toughest part of bold thinking...dislodging the notion that the business owner has to work harder than everyone else.

But it is essential in order to attain personal freedom. You'll need to work on this one.

Intolerance

Weak-minded business owners accept poor performance from employees.

You *cannot tolerate* employees who believe *they* run the business, who believe they are empowered to ignore the owner's directives, or who undermine the business through their actions.

It takes courage to confront employees who are damaging your business—especially if they are long-term employees or relatives (yikes!). But it's absolutely necessary.

You must enforce the business practices that you have established. If employees refuse to adhere to your directions, then they have to go.

Be bold. Be intolerant.

Salesmanship

Napoleon Hill, author of *Think and Grow Rich*, said, "It is exceedingly rare to find a wealthy person—unless by inheritance—who has not made himself or herself into a master salesman."

Advertising, marketing, and sales are considered "dark arts" by too many business owners. Mastering the sales process—and how to make closing the sale a natural progression of the process—is absolutely necessary.

But it is overlooked by most contractors. It's not a stretch to say that, if you adopt six of the seven points I've outlined in this chapter but leave out salesmanship, your likelihood of success drops dramatically.

Think about this…

Advertising and marketing are really nothing more than selling in print. The better you are at selling, the more impactful your advertising and marketing will be.

We'll talk more about your selling process in chapter 15.

There's a quote I love by Goethe that ends this way: "Boldness has genius, power, and magic in it."

I truly believe that a boldness mind-set will lead you to every goal you've ever dreamed about.

It's worth working on.

SECTION III
Backwards Marketing

CHAPTER 11

Marketing Strategies to Drive Growth in Sales and Profits

In this third section, I'm going to zero in on specific methods, strategies, and processes that you can use in your business to drive lead flow, revenue, and profits.

If that sounds good to you, then keep reading.

Remember back at the very beginning of this book when I said that most advertising and marketing done by contractors is awful? Well, my opinion hasn't changed since then. In fact, I'm going to add here that most contractors are clueless when it comes to advertising and marketing. If you've been feeling that you don't know where to start or how exactly to market your business, you're not alone.

Still, the fact remains that, if you want to stay in business, you need customers...and plenty of them. No matter how good you are at your craft, how attentive to your customers' needs, or how many hours a day you work, if your phone isn't ringing, you're going to be out of business in a pretty short time. That's the cold, hard truth.

So you need to get your name and your company out there so that prospective customers can find you. At the same time, I'm guessing you don't have a whole lot of extra money to sink into marketing that isn't doing its job or isn't doing it very well. Not an easy challenge for any business owner.

Backwards Marketing

I'm going to start this section by talking about how you can make a huge breakthrough in your business by doing something very simple with your marketing and advertising. Just do the opposite of what everyone else is doing—engage in *backwards marketing*!

I'm not kidding.

My prescription for your success is to switch from copying what almost everyone is doing and start copying some of the junk mail that you get. In other words, switch from ordinary traditional marketing to *direct-response* marketing.

Most small businesses copy what everyone else in their industry is doing. Tell me the truth…When you were planning your Yellow Pages ad, or designing your website, or writing a newspaper or Valpak ad, or a flyer or door hanger, you looked at what others in your industry were doing, didn't you? And then you pretty much just replaced their name and logo with yours, and perhaps used a different color scheme in designing your own advertising, right? It's a good bet that you said yes to those questions.

Or did you allow the ad reps to design your ad—or the web guy to write the copy for your website? That's even worse.

You see, almost every small business puts out "image" advertisements. These ads have your logo at the top, usually a picture or two of some projects you did, some bullet points about your services, and your phone number and website address. Maybe you have statements like "Family Owned and Operated" or "Satisfaction Guaranteed" as well. If you're really creative, you have a coupon.

Sound familiar?

Your ad looks the same as everyone else's ad because that's all the ad reps know how to do. And the idea that you need to run an ad five to ten times so that people have multiple "impressions" is just baloney. Why in the world would these people up and decide to call you just because they saw your ad for the fifth time, when they weren't really interested in calling you after they saw your ad the first time?

It's all such a huge waste of money. It works out great for the people selling the ads, but not so great for you.

Now, you might be thinking that you see a lot of big companies that do this kind of advertising, and they didn't get that big or that successful by doing the wrong kind of advertising.

Well, you're right. Big companies spend millions and millions of dollars doing image advertising to build their brands, their positioning, and their presence in certain markets. But you have to recognize that large corporations have very different goals for their advertising than small businesses do. And they have much deeper pockets.

Their goals, among others, are to please their shareholders, look good to their investors and to their industry peers, build their brand identities, and win awards for the creativity of their advertising. Oh yeah...and maybe they want to make sales someday.

Your goal is what? To sell something. Soon.

The Magic of Direct Marketing

So what is *direct marketing*? Very simply, direct marketing—or more exactly, *direct-response marketing*—is a style of advertising that grabs your target prospects' attention and motivates them to respond immediately. By "immediately" I mean you send your ad out today, and your phone starts ringing tomorrow.

Direct marketing calls for your ads to be tracked and measured so that you can see which ones are working, which are delivering profitable customers to you, which you should spend more on, and which you should drop. You do that by applying the lessons you learned about in The Importance of Marketing Math.

The good news is that writing direct-marketing ads is no more difficult than writing traditional image ads. In fact, it can be a lot more fun.

In the next chapter, I'll go into detail about how to write great ads, but you need to face the fact that no one else can ever write your ads or marketing pieces again. You know more about your business and your industry than any ad rep or web designer. You need to write your own ads.

I'm going to outline for you a few basic components of a direct-response ad. As I said before, we're going to look in detail at writing ads in the next chapter, but it's important that you understand the basic structure.

And keep in mind that advertisements come in all shapes, sizes, and formats, so these principles apply not only to ads but also to sales letters, door hangers, postcards, websites, flyers, e-mails, and any other marketing you do. For now we're just going to use the term "ad" to refer to them all.

Here is the formula for a great direct-response ad:

1. Your ad must start with a bold headline that provokes interest.
2. It makes an irresistible offer.
3. It creates interest by educating the reader about the offer and your product or service.
4. It creates desire by giving the reader lots of benefits.
5. It always includes a strong call to action and creates urgency with a deadline to respond.

Upon this basic structure are built most of the great advertisements and sales letters. There are other "tricks of the trade" that are also used, which we'll talk about more, but if you structure a marketing piece with these components and send it to the right market, you will dramatically increase your likelihood of success.

Where to Find Inspiration for Your Marketing

I encourage you to start loving your mailbox. There's an education worth millions being delivered by the postman every day. You see, the folks who develop this kind of mail are often very accomplished marketers. They know and use this formula. Instead of throwing all that "junk mail" out, keep it, study it, copy it, and profit from it.

And don't think that you need to look for advertisements and marketing only from within your own industry or even only from contractors. Oftentimes, the best ideas come from completely unrelated industries. Inspiration for your next great marketing piece could come from a dry cleaner, an insurance agent, a dentist, a jewelry store, or even an accountant.

Advertising legend David Ogilvy said, "It takes a big idea to attract the attention of consumers and get them to buy your product. Unless your advertising contains a big idea, it will pass like a ship in the night. I doubt if more than one campaign in a hundred contains a big idea."

Let me give you an example of how you can take an idea from another industry and make it your "big idea." One of my mentors in marketing, Dan Kennedy, includes in his brilliant book *The Ultimate Sales Letter* a series of marketing letters to be used by a restaurant. These are often called the "Giorgio letters."

Let's take a look at the first letter in his series and see how we could use it to inspire an ad for a home-remodeling business.

At the end of this chapter, I have reprinted Dan Kennedy's letter—which he has given me permission to use—and following it, my version of the letter that a home-remodeling contractor could use. Go ahead and have a look at them now.

I think you'll agree that the original Giorgio letter is brilliant. There's a reason that Dan Kennedy is one of the highest-paid copywriters in the world and has a waiting list of clients who are desperate to pay him incredible sums of money to develop a marketing letter or campaign.

You'll see that he has used all of the components from the formula. By the way, this letter is the first in a series of three letters. Sending a series of letters is a marketing strategy devised by Dan Kennedy and has proven to be incredibly effective in dozens and dozens of industries. You really owe it to yourself to get his book *The Ultimate Sales Letter*.

Now look at how we "borrowed" the concept. With just a few changes, we've taken a sales letter used by a restaurant and turned it into a sales letter for a home-remodeling contractor.

I like to call that my "R&D" writing method—repurpose and distribute. Now, you have to use this method ethically; you can't copy exactly what someone else has done, especially if it's in your industry. But you can borrow a concept and change it to fit what you want to sell. It's a great way to get ideas and inspiration for your own marketing campaigns.

In fact, even the great copywriters who make their living writing sales letters and marketing pieces collect examples of marketing that works. These are called "swipe files," and that's exactly what they're used for—to swipe ideas.

Warning – You *Will* Be Criticized

When you start doing direct-response marketing, your ads and marketing pieces will look very different from what others are doing. It'll go against the grain of established norms and conventions in your industry. Ad reps, peers in your industry, your partners—heck, even your family—will question you...They'll tell you it won't work.

Your wife may secretly hope that her friends don't see your ads.

Remember, only *you* will know whether a specific marketing strategy or campaign is successful or not, because you'll be tracking it. Think about it. Ad reps don't really want you to know how the ad you're running in their media is doing, because then you gain control.

How would the Yellow Pages rep react if, next year, you presented him with your ROI on the ad you placed compared with other marketing you did, and told *him* how much you were willing to pay for your ad? I think you'll agree that you'll be in the better bargaining position.

You must be strong. You cannot bend to the opinions of others. If you consistently apply the methods and strategies I have laid out for you in this book, your marketing will succeed. In the end, those who criticized you will want to copy you. And then who will be laughing?

Focus on Your Results

I wish I knew who said this, but it's a great saying: "Successful people are more interested in pleasing results than in pleasing methods."

Focus on your results. Be immune to criticism of your methods. When you lay your head on your pillow at night, rather than worrying whether the phone will ring tomorrow, you'll know with certainty that your marketing is out there doing its work while you sleep.

That, my friend, is called peace of mind, and its value cannot be measured.

<Insert a Picture

of Yourself>

A Confidential Letter to the Husband of the House from Giorgio

"She may be waiting... just anticipating... things she may never possess... but while she's waiting, try a little tenderness..."

April 16th

Dear Husband,

Women are different than we are. (Vive le difference!) YOUR loving wife needs, wants, and deserves SPECIAL ATTENTION maybe more often than you think to give it to her.

You are busy. Preoccupied with work. Aggravated with that dumb-dumb you have to deal with every day at the office. Tired. Who has time or the energy to even think about "romance?" (Two-thirds of all marriages end in divorce and the number-one reason given by divorcing women—"he just didn't pay enough attention to me anymore.")

For you, my friend, I have got a SOLUTION!

With this letter, YOU are entitled to an evening charmed by all the creativity of Giorgio, the Official Romance Director!

When you and your Very-Significant-Other arrive at Giorgio's, you'll be ushered into the special dining room lit only by candlelight and the roaring fire in the fireplace... with the view of the sunset or starry night over the harbor! (When you make your reservation, I will GUARANTEE your choice of a near-the-fireplace or window-side table!)

In this uncrowded, intimate dining room there will be NO families, NO CHILDREN, NO disruptions.

Quiet mood music. A peaceful environment. A haven from the hustle, bustle, noise, and pushing and shoving and rushing of the real world.

On your table, in a crystal bud vase, there will be a single dewy-fresh red rose for your lady. (It and the vase are hers to take home.)

We will begin with a carafe of our wonderful house Italian wine—red or white, your choice—compliments of Giorgio! And freshly baked, piping hot, lightly garlic-buttered, crusty Italian breadsticks.

For dinner, all the TENDERNESS the two of you can handle—if you choose the specialty of the house: an entrée of melt-in-your-mouth tender veal on a bed of angel hair pasta, with to-die-for pesto sauce... or your choice of five other wonderful entrees.

Any choice from our dessert tray...

Espresso...

And finally a heart shaped box with four delicate, Italian gelato filled chocolates presented to your lady with a flourish!

Now, is that an evening to enjoy, to luxuriate in, to remember? Will that make you a hero? AH—Giorgio GUARANTEES it.

We can only accommodate twelve couples each evening with this very special Romance Dinner, so it's important to call and make reservations as early as you can. Ask for me—Giorgio— Noon to 10:00 P.M. (or stop in for our Businessman's lunch). See me, and make these Romance arrangements personally. I'm the handsome-looking devil in the deep blue tuxedo jacket, in the lounge.

Awaiting your commands—to make a'magic for you!

Giorgio

P.S. The cost? EVERYTHING, the entire Romance Dinner for two, exactly as I've described it—just $59.95. If you wish you can even pay in advance with your VISA, MASTERCARD, AMERICAN EXPRESS, or CARTE BLANCHE and not be troubled by a check the evening you are here.

<Insert a Picture

of Yourself>

A Confidential Letter to the Husband of the House from Giorgio

"She may be waiting...just anticipating... things she may never possess...but while she's waiting, try a little tenderness..."

April 16

Dear Husband,

Women are different than we are. (Vive le difference!) YOUR loving wife needs, wants, and deserves a SPECIAL LUXURY maybe more often than you think to give it to her.

You are busy. Preoccupied with work. Aggravated with that dumb-dumb you have to deal with every day at the office. Tired. Who has time or the energy to even think about "romance"? (Two-thirds of all marriages end in divorce and the number-one reason given by divorcing women—"He just didn't pay enough attention to me anymore.")

For you, my friend, I have a SOLUTION!

Is there anything that a woman loves more than a luxurious master bath? (Has she been feeling neglected because her friends have these extravagances?)

Imagine for a moment, when your Very-Significant-Other enters her private sanctuary, she'll be stepping into her own special retreat, lit only by candlelight...surrounded by exquisite Italian tile, beautiful hand-carved woodwork, and immaculate new fixtures! She will immerse herself in a gorgeous tub filled with fragrantly perfumed water, hot...but not too hot. Perhaps she will switch on a gentle stream of bubbles to caress her body.

In this calm, intimate setting, there will be NO families, NO CHILDREN, NO disruptions. Quiet mood music. A peaceful environment. A haven from the hustle, bustle, noise, and pushing and shoving and rushing of the real world.

On the marble vanity, in a crystal bud vase, there will be a single dewy-fresh red rose for your lady.

With this letter, YOU are entitled to a luxury master bath design, conceived with all the creativity of Giorgio, the Official Romance Director!

When you contact me directly, we will arrange a time to meet with you and your Beloved. We want to be certain that we take into account her desires... her wants. Our specialty is the design of home spaces that offer a calm and relaxing refuge from the world outside. We also specialize in making the construction process easy and stress-free for you.

Our professional designer will help you choose just the right fixtures, the perfect tile and marble, the exact shade of paint to complement your choices. We will not leave you and your loving wife to struggle with these decisions by yourselves.

We employ only the most capable and skilled craftsmen so that you are assured of the very highest quality result. We also carefully screen our employees so that your adoring wife need never worry who is coming and going from your home.

And finally, we stand behind our work with our ironclad warranty! You will both be absolutely delighted with your new master bath.

Now, will that make you a hero? AHH—Giorgio GUARANTEES it.

We can only accommodate twelve homeowners with this very special Romance Package—which must be scheduled before May 15—so it's important to call and make arrangements as early as you can. Ask for me—Giorgio—8:00 a.m. to 6:00 p.m. (And if you feel that your Beloved would prefer a new kitchen or sunroom, then we will extend this Romance offer to those projects as well.)

Awaiting your commands—to make a'magic for you!

Giorgio

PS: The cost? EVERYTHING—the entire design for your new master bath, kitchen, or sunroom exactly as I've described it—just $259. If you wish, you can even pay with your VISA, MASTERCARD, or AMERICAN EXPRESS.

CHAPTER 12

The Quick and Easy Way to Create Great Ads

I n chapter 11 I said that you can no longer allow advertising reps to write your ads or web designers to write the copy for your website. You must create your own marketing.

I know that for a lot of contractors, that's a tall order. So, in this chapter, I'm going to give you a paint-by-numbers process to help you write your own advertisements and marketing pieces.

This chapter is longer than the others because we cover a lot of ground. The information contained here pulls together a lot of what I've covered in the book so far, so it's really important. Please take the time to read it and understand it. You may even want to read it more than once.

Market-Message-Media Triangle Revisited

Let's take just a moment to review the market-message-media triangle from chapter 1. We said that you need to make decisions in the following order:

1. Select your target market, ideally one that will allow you to prosper.

2. Determine a marketing message that will appeal to your target market on an emotional level.
3. Choose the media to efficiently and affordably reach your target market.

This fundamental concept is critical to have in mind when you set out to create a marketing piece.

The first step in creating your own marketing is to know what your objective is. Now, I know that your objective is to increase sales, but I'm talking about your objective for the marketing piece. This is a critically important point that most marketers get wrong. They try to get their ad to sell their product or service, which is absolutely the wrong approach.

Think about it. There's only so much you can say in an ad. If I told you that you had to give your whole sales presentation in under five minutes, you'd tell me I'm nuts. It's the same thing with advertising. You can't possibly sell anyone in the space you have in a typical ad. So we need to have a different goal for the ad.

The objective of your ad or marketing piece is to generate a response from a qualified lead.

That's it.

Whether you want people to go to your website, call your office, click on a link in an e-mail, watch a video, whatever, the goal of your marketing is to get them to take that first small step toward becoming customers. By taking that step, they raise their hands and express interest in the product or service that you sell…They've moved themselves from anonymous members of your target market, and they are now leads.

That's a good thing for you.

Now, in order to get them to raise their hands, we have to offer them something. But what?

Back in chapter 3, I talked about crafting your message to appeal to your market on an emotional level, and in chapter 4, I talked about offering a consumer education piece to your target market. It might be a good idea to go back and read those chapters again right now. It'll only take a couple of minutes.

Now, do me a favor and grab a recent copy of your local newspaper. If you don't have one, grab the Yellow Pages. Find the section where contractors place ads. In my local newspaper, they're in a section called "Hire a Professional." If you have the Yellow Pages, just open to the section that has your ad—or would have your ad if you're not in the Yellow Pages.

What do you notice about the ads that you see? They all look essentially the same, don't they? And most—probably all—of them look like the ads I described in the last chapter...company name at the top, bullets describing what they do, and some general platitudes like "Satisfaction Guaranteed" or "Locally Owned."

If you went back and read chapters 3 and 4, the strategy should be getting clearer to you. While all of your competitors are running copycat ads that are trying to sell their services, you're going to advertise your consumer information piece. You'll be the only one offering advice and information to buyers to help them make better decisions. Can you see how this changes the game in your favor?

Now that we have that clear, let's talk about writing the ad itself. Again, if you've paid attention to your mailbox, you may get some great inspiration.

Writing a Bold Headline That Provokes Interest

A headline for an ad is just what it sounds like. Your marketing piece is going to look a lot like an article in the newspaper, and a headline is always at the top of an article.

Even your sales letters are going to have headlines. I'm well aware that letters don't usually have headlines, but successful sales letters do.

The purpose of the headline is to catch and hold the readers' attention and demand that they read the rest of the ad. Your headline must make an immediate impression on readers about what your offer is going to do for them.

Ideally, you want the headline to reach out and grab the individual reader and say to that person, "Hey, John…this is for *you*!" Of course, that's not really possible, but we try to get as close to this ideal as we can.

A heating-and-air-conditioning contractor in my local area had an interesting headline that read, "Your Wife is HOT!" That certainly grabs your attention. I assume the ad was for AC service. I say that because it was on a billboard, and it was impossible to read the ad copy as I was racing past on the interstate. Good headline, bad choice of medium.

That headline could work for a pool and spa builder, couldn't it?

When writing headlines, I like to ask: What's the biggest benefit the prospect will get by responding to this offer? In the answer to that question lies the headline.

For example, let's say you decide to offer a kitchen or bath "refresh" as an alternative to having a full-blown kitchen remodel. You might write this headline, "Discover the Secret of a Beautiful, Updated Kitchen or Bath While Slashing Your Remodeling Costs in Half!" Now, if readers have been thinking about a kitchen remodel or have a dated kitchen, how can they *not* read the rest of the ad?

When writing a headline, think about what might be of interest to your target market. Consider the following:

- Promise a benefit or provoke curiosity.
- If possible, put the name of the offer or product in the headline.
- Long headlines often get better response than short headlines.
- Don't make it confusing; stick to one main idea or offer.

- Words like "new," "free," "how to," "amazing," "introducing," "guaranteed," and "you" all work well in headlines.
- Don't make the reader think too much.
- Make it believable.
- Testimonials can work very well as headlines.
- Solve a problem.
- Fulfill a dream.

Another thing I like to do when writing a headline is to imagine myself as a door-to-door salesman. I just knocked on someone's door, and when the door is opened, I'm going to say my headline. What's their response? Is it "Wow, tell me more about that," or is it "Who cares?"

Let me give you an example of a weak headline: "Would You Like a Pool?" That's no good. It's too easy for the reader to say, "No thanks."

Here's another one: "George's Painting—I Paint Homes." That's not a headline that's going to get any sort of decent response or make you any money.

How can we make those headlines more interesting and compelling? How about this: "Can a New Swimming Pool Enrich Your Family Life?" Or, "Can Lighter, Brighter Wall Colors Affect Your Happiness and Quality of Life?"

Aren't these a lot more interesting? Don't they make you want to read the rest of the story? Isn't the homeowner less likely to slam the door on your foot? I hope you get the idea.

If you've gone on YouTube recently, you've noticed that they often-times have an ad that plays before you can watch the video you want to watch. But most of these video ads have a little spot that you can click to skip the ad after the first few seconds. I've become addicted to seeing what these ads do in the first few seconds to make me want to watch the rest of the video ad. It's a great lesson in capturing attention.

There are several good sources for headlines that I like to use. I get my high-speed Internet at home through Comcast, and I have several e-mail accounts with them. Every time I go to the main website to log in to my e-mail, there are a bunch of "news" stories, personal interest stories, entertainment news, sports, and other stuff there. The headlines are designed to grab your attention so that you'll read the story or click on a link or watch a video.

Sound familiar? We can use these headlines as inspiration.

As I was writing this, I opened up the website, and one headline that popped out at me was "Fifteen Natural Remedies for Back Pain." Now, how can we use that as inspiration for a headline? How about..."Local Contractor Offers Remedy for Back Pain"? The sales letter could offer information on ways to design your kitchen and bath counter heights to relieve back pain.

Or, for a pool and spa contractor, it could offer information about how swimming relieves back pain.

Another headline from the Comcast site: "'Healthy' Foods You Shouldn't be Eating." Let's rework this one for our purposes. How about this..."'Trendy' Kitchen Designs You Shouldn't Be Copying." Or, "'Natural' Landscape Trends You Shouldn't be Copying."

Sometimes you'll come across headlines that are already perfect that you can simply use unchanged. Two headlines were like that today.

"Kitchen Remodel: When to Splurge, Save." You can use that one just as it is.

"Pro Shares Money-Saving Construction Tips." Again, no change needed on this one.

Let's try changing one more just for the fun of it.

First, the headline I saw: "Ten Powerful Cars of the Last Decade."

Now, revised for our purposes: "Ten Stunning Kitchen Designs of Last Year."

Or "Ten Stunning Pools of Last Year."

Or "Ten Inspirational Color Schemes of Last Year."

Or "Ten Incredible Landscape Designs of Last Year."

Do you see how easy it is?

Magazines are another great source for inspiration, especially health and women's magazines.

The next time you're in a grocery store or convenience mart, take a look at *Ladies' Home Journal, Good Housekeeping, Reader's Digest, Prevention*, and, especially, *Cosmopolitan*. The covers have great headlines for the articles contained within. Their job is to get the shopper to pick up and buy the magazine, so they have to be compelling and create interest very quickly.

Some copywriters I know subscribe to these publications. They rip off and save the covers for their swipe files, and throw the rest of the magazine into the recycling bin.

Make an Irresistible Offer

From chapter 4, which you just read again, you'll recall that we talked in detail about creating consumer information to help people select the best contractor for them. You're positioning yourself as the contractor who's on *their* side, not the one who's just trying to sell them.

So this information is what I want you to offer to your target market. Now, it's possible that your consumer report is going to be effective for a very long time, which will be great for you. The likelihood, though, is that you'll need to change it slightly from time to time.

For example, remember the headline I showed you earlier, "Do Lighter, Brighter Wall Colors Affect Your Happiness and Your Quality of Life?" What you would do is add a new section to your consumer information report about research that was done that proves that lighter, brighter wall colors positively impact mood. The rest of the consumer information would remain the same, focusing on picking the best contractor, which of course is you.

The same goes for the other headline, "Can a New Swimming Pool Enrich Your Family Life?" Again, you would add a section about the pool lifestyle and how families with pools spend more time together.

See how easy that is?

Your industry and association publications contain plenty of information about research and evidence that you can use to create your ads and change your offer from time to time. So you don't need to look too far for inspiration.

More Ways to Create Offers

Now, I firmly believe that high-quality, reputable contractors should charge premium prices, and I'm generally not in favor of discounting. But, if you decide to create a special offer—which might be smart to fill in a slow season or test a new service that you're thinking about—then you would want to advertise that special offer.

Let's say, for instance, that winter is a slow season for your home-remodeling business. You decide to create an offer to fill in this slow time.

First, you want to see whether your suppliers have any special pricing going on. Perhaps a product line has been discontinued or a supplier has overstocked a product that you can get good pricing on. You can create special offers around these discounts, and it's always great if you can say that you're passing your savings on to the customer.

The best offers are similar to what you see in retail stores, so you might offer:

- buy two kitchen cabinets, get the third free;
- buy one kitchen cabinet, get a second at half off;
- I'll buy the granite slab for your new kitchen; or
- free kitchen cabinet upgrade.

Of course, anytime you have pricing that's different than your regular pricing, it's crucial that you know your lifetime customer value so that you can structure your offer without putting a huge dent in your long-term profits.

Create Interest by Educating the Reader about the Offer

As I said earlier, the job of the headline is to get the reader to read the first sentence of your ad. Now that you've accomplished that, you need to be sure the first sentence gets them to read the next one...and that sentence to read the following one.

You want the reader to get your whole message. And in order to do that, you need to keep this in mind: *you cannot be boring*. Your copy must be interesting. It has to be different than what the reader expects from a contractor. Make it fun. You have to charm prospects and hold their interest. If you bore them, they'll be gone.

And remember to focus on *their* needs and desires. Get rid of every "I" and replace it with a "you." Speak to the reader personally. Don't say, "Everyone who responds to this offer..." Rather, say, "When you respond to this offer..." You want them to feel like they're having a conversation with you...just the two of you.

Keep in mind that most people know very little about what you do. Whether you're a pavement contractor, a roofer, a home remodeler or custom home builder, a landscaper, a pool and spa contractor, a painter, or any other kind of contractor, your prospects are clueless about what goes into completing a quality project. They don't even know what questions to ask, much less how to pick the best contractor for their project.

But they want to hire trustworthy contractors and get the best value. So you need to focus your copy on answering their questions—even if they don't know what the right questions are. And the most important question to answer is "What's in it for me?"

It's critical that you put yourself in your prospects' shoes. Although you are writing the ad, you have to remember that you're not the prospect. It's not always easy to do.

Something that seems obvious to you may be completely new information to your prospects. I once made the mistake of having a handyman paint a bathroom for me. I was at my office while he was doing the work, so I didn't see what he was doing, but it seemed like he was done pretty quickly.

Well, I learned the hard way why using the right primer, the right kind of paint, and applying multiple coats rather than one heavy coat are important, especially in a bathroom. The professional painter I hired to redo the job explained all that to me. Had the professional painter offered a consumer education report about these things beforehand, there's a good chance I would've had him do the painting the first time around rather than let the handyman do it.

What specifics about your business or industry are the public unaware of? Are there any "common myths" that you want to set people straight about?

When you have lunch with your dentist or accountant, as I suggested earlier, you might ask them what questions they would have if they were getting ready to hire a contractor like you.

They might say, "You know, I've always wondered why some cabinets cost three times as much as other cabinets. Is there really that much of a difference?"

Or, "Why is it that, when I plant a bush, it always dies? What's the secret?"

You'll get a lot of insight from having these conversations, and that will give you topics for your consumer report and your advertising and marketing.

Create Desire by Giving the Reader Lots of Benefits

I touched on this topic earlier but want to go deeper.

Most contractors focus on features in their advertising. They do that because, to them, the benefits are obvious. But they're not obvious to your target market. When you show readers benefits, it triggers hidden response mechanisms that actually make prospects want to contact you.

I think the best way to illustrate this is to look at some examples. Let's take some of the things I see in contractor advertising all the time, and turn them from feature statements into benefits.

Here's one: "In Business for Eighteen Years."

Now, put yourself in your customer's shoes and ask, "Why should that matter to me?"

You might answer that it matters because your customer can have confidence that you'll be around to keep up your end of the warranty if something does go wrong.

Great. We're on the right track.

So, now we're going to say, "You can trust that we'll be here to repair any issues that may arise with your project in the future." That's a benefit.

Do you see the difference?

Okay, how about "Satisfaction Guaranteed"? An old standby. This is one that has lost its meaning because everyone says it.

Instead, you should say, "Our skilled, experienced craftsmen have been delighting your neighbors for eighteen years." Can you see how that's a benefit?

Let's try another oldie, "Family Owned and Operated."

Why should I care?

How about this? "We are a family-owned company, and we don't answer to any corporation or out-of-town investors who might want us to cut corners on your project to increase their profits. We measure our success by the contentment of our customers."

Wow. That's a good one!

Okay, the last one I'll look at is the one I hate most: "Revolutionary Contracting—We Paint Homes." Or, "...We Do Kitchens and Baths." Or, "...We Install Pools." Or, "...We Do Landscaping."

These really get my goat because they're so unimaginative. I probably shouldn't let it bother me, but it does. And they're obviously not benefits.

How about these benefits instead?

"Your home will pop with vibrancy as a result of our six-step painting process."

"Your kitchen is sure to be a welcoming retreat for your family and friends with our certified design process."

"Our unique installation process is guaranteed to make your pool the envy of the neighborhood."

"Beautify and increase the value of your home with our guaranteed easy-care landscape-design process. If you spend more than an hour a week maintaining your yard, we'll refund every cent."

Don't you agree that these statements are much more likely to create desire in your prospects than the feature statements you're using now?

Always Include a Strong Call to Action and Create Urgency

You're probably familiar with the call to action from television commercials you've seen or radio commercials you've heard.

They sound something like this, "Call before midnight, and instead of one whiz-bang bottle of gunk-cleaning glop, we'll send you two."

Or, "This special offer absolutely ends at midnight on April twenty-ninth."

That's difficult to do in our world, unless you've developed an offer based on special pricing from a supplier, which we talked about earlier. In that case, you should definitely use either a time or limited-quantity call to action.

But you need to create urgency in your prospects so that they don't set aside your ad for "whenever." You have to make sure they take action and respond now.

The easiest way to have a call to action is to simply say, "Go ahead and pick up the phone right now, and call us at 555-555-5555!" Believe it or not, even this simple statement will increase the response to your marketing. Sometimes, you just have to tell people what to do, and they'll do it.

What works well in the contracting world is a limited number of slots that you have available. I know a painter that runs a campaign every fall to fill up his otherwise slow winter season. His call to action is simply that he has a certain number of jobs he can do, and once the slots are gone, the offer is gone. He never has a slow winter.

You can also borrow from those late-night TV shows and create urgency by having a bonus offer: "The first eight people who call to schedule their pool installation get a full year of maintenance and cleaning absolutely free."

Obviously you have to work out the economics in order to make that offer work.

Summarizing this admittedly long chapter, every time you create an ad, put yourself in your prospects' shoes. Then use this chapter as a guide to creating your ad.

CHAPTER 13

Care and Feeding of Your Customers

'll bet if you owned an automobile dealership rather than a contracting business, you'd pay a lot more attention to staying in touch with your customers and keeping them engaged.

After all, in the dealership business, they depend on customers coming back again and again in order to stay in business. If they sold a car or a truck to each customer only once, they'd run through their potential customer base pretty quickly, don't you think?

Same goes for restaurants. If you have a local restaurant that does a good job of marketing, I'll bet they regularly send you offers trying to get you to come through the door more often. It makes sense.

For some reason, contractors almost never stay in touch with their customers.

Some years ago, shortly after I bought my home, I saw some carpenter ants inside the house. Having heard that, if you see one, there are probably a hundred inside the wall, I immediately called an exterminator.

The guy came and treated my house. I liked him. His truck was nice and clean, he was very personable, he was careful to keep my house clean, and he was a local business, which I tend to prefer. Then he left, and I never heard from him again.

A year or so later, I wanted to get set up with regular treatments for my house, but I couldn't for the life of me remember the guy's name or the name of his company. How I wished I could find his information. Eventually I hired a different company for the maintenance treatments. They've been treating my house for fourteen years. I'm a pretty nice account for them.

You may be thinking, okay, for a service contractor like an exterminator, it makes sense to stay in touch with clients. But why would remodelers or painters or other project-oriented contractors make a big effort to stay in touch with their customers?

That's what we're going to talk about in this chapter. Some of the ideas I talked about in earlier chapters could just as well have been in this chapter, like the customer appreciation event or the vacation postcard.

Your Most Valuable Asset

Your past customers are your single most valuable asset. They're worth more to you than your vehicles and equipment, more than your shop or building, even more than your employees.

Why?

Well, for one thing—and take note...this is huge—they have the ability to give you referrals. We already talked about why that's important. But here's something you probably didn't consider: every month that goes by without maintaining your relationship with your past customers, they become 10 percent less likely to refer you.

After about a year, if you've done nothing to stay connected with your customers, there's almost no chance that they'll refer you.

Think about it...Let's say you had dinner at a terrific restaurant a few weeks ago, and your neighbor is asking about a nice restaurant. You're likely to tell them what a nice time you had. But, if you had that nice dinner a year or two ago, are you likely to mention that restaurant?

Probably not. Why? Because who knows what might have changed in the meantime. Maybe the chef left. The service, which was great then, might be lousy now. It happens. And, besides that, you've had several other nice dinners more recently, and those restaurants are fresher in your mind.

You see…time kills relationships.

Another important point here is that "like refers like." In other words, good customers tend to refer good customers, and cheapskate customers tend to refer cheapskates.

You've targeted the kind of people you want as clients and done all the hard work of creating a marketing message that speaks to them and their desires. By staying connected to your customers, you'll create a river of referrals that are right in your target market.

Do you want a flood of targeted referrals?

Here's another reason to stay in touch with your customers: they might have other projects they want you to do.

In the fifteen years that I've owned my home, I've had six sizeable re-modeling projects done:

1. I bumped out the front of my living room and put in a fireplace.
2. I had my basement finished.
3. I had my kitchen and adjoining powder room fully remodeled.
4. I had all of my windows replaced and new siding and a new roof put on.
5. I've had my master bedroom turned into a suite, including bumping out over my garage to create a huge walk-in closet.
6. I've had my two upstairs bathrooms completely remodeled.

Guess how many contractors I've had for those six projects?

That's right…six.

Maybe you think I'm a disloyal customer. Why didn't I use even one of the contractors again?

I must admit it's hard to say. But here's how it happened…Two didn't really treat us that well as customers. One started another big job about halfway through my project, and our relationship ended badly. But three of them, had they bothered to keep in touch with me, I would have hired again.

Basically, I was neglected.

For our last project—which was the two bathroom remodels—we chose the contractor because he had done a similar bathroom remodel for a neighbor of ours. No special reason, really.

My point is that, had the remodeler who'd done the first project—the living room bump out—stayed in touch with us, we probably would have hired him to do all of the projects. He worked for us almost fifteen years ago, and I've never heard a single word from him since he packed up his tools and collected his final payment.

It has cost him, to the tune of about $230,000, and I'm sure he doesn't even realize it.

And I've never seen his truck or heard of him doing any other work in my neighborhood, so he obviously didn't communicate in any way with my neighbors about the work he did at my house. He's never asked me for a testimonial or to be a reference for him.

As my fourteen-year-old kid says, "Total failure!"

The Treasure Buried in Your Business

Business owners are taught to always be looking for new customers. But there's a gold mine hiding right in your file cabinets. Is there any doubt that at least some of your past customers are looking to do another job right now? Or they have a neighbor, friend, family member, or work associate that they know is getting ready to hire a contractor like you?

You and I both know the answer to that question. The real question is, will they call you? Or refer you?

I'm guessing you think they will. You might even think they *owe* it to you to refer you.

But other contractors are trying to lure your customers away from you every day. They're working in the neighborhoods where you want to work, doing jobs you want, and getting referrals of their own from their customers. If they're smart, they're sending letters and making special offers to the whole neighborhood, and your customers are getting those letters and offers.

I'm telling you, if your customers feel ignored or unappreciated, you open the door for your competitors to steal them. If they haven't heard from you in six or twelve months, they're not your customers anymore.

The key is to build a glass wall around your customers so that they're immune to the overtures of your competitors, so that they immediately think of you and only you when they are contemplating their next project, and so that they'll always mention your name when talking about a great contractor.

Your goal is to establish a personal relationship with them.

You do this by communicating with them—frequently. I believe that "touching" your customers at least twenty-four times a year is the absolute minimum. Fifty-two times a year is better. And that doesn't include sales letters or specific offers.

"No way…that's *way* too much. My customers are gonna be ticked off if I send them something that often. I don't want to bother them…"

I just read your mind, didn't I?

There's a fitness business in my town that my wife went to for a three-week intro package a few years ago. They've sent two or three e-mails a week to us ever since. I read most of the e-mails because they're funny, informative, inspirational, clever, and give good advice…In other words, *they're* not *boring*.

And that's the key. Just like your other marketing, you must be interesting. If you bore your customers, or only send them something when you want to sell them, then your messages will become unwelcome. Otherwise, it's almost impossible to communicate with them too much.

By the way, the fitness business finally got me by offering a nutrition program just about the time I was thinking I needed to lose twenty pounds. If they hadn't sent those e-mails, I would never have known about or enrolled in their program.

The Number One Marketing Tool in Your Arsenal

The number one method I recommend to communicate with your customer base is to launch a program and send something to your customers in the mail every month.

I know…I know. You've heard this advice before.

And I've given the advice before. I can tell you all the excuses why you don't want to do it.

**Excuse Number One – "It's so much work…
Do I have to do this every month?"**

Yes. Not every other month. Not quarterly. This is the primary tool you will use to build a personal relationship with your customers. And they need to hear from you more often than every two or three months.

Think about reality TV shows. I believe these shows are so popular in part because we all have fewer close friends these days. Instead of having a beer with our neighbor, we have these people show up in our homes once a week via the TV. They become our friends.

Who hasn't felt a connection with one or another of the participants on *Biggest Loser*? We root for them. We want them to win the competitions. We want them to work hard and shed all of those pounds. We want them to find love and happiness.

Now, if you're like most people, maybe especially contractors, you're a little uncomfortable with the idea of revealing a lot of personal information to your customers. Well, you won't have to. But you will have to entertain them, inform them, and share at least a little bit about you, your family, your hobbies, and your opinions.

You can get a formula to easily create your own monthly mailer program on this book's website, www.bernieheer.com.

It may seem odd to you, but you want to put yourself in very much the same situation as the reality TV stars. Your customers will know a whole lot more about you than you know about them. They'll care about you. You'll be their "friend" even though they're not really *your* friends.

Another thing…believe it or not, it's harder to do a mailer quarterly than it is to do it monthly.

When you commit yourself to doing a monthly mailer, you are constantly on the lookout for articles or material you can use. You'll have a drawer or a basket that you stick this stuff into, and when it's time to write the newsletter, it's easy to do.

When you do it less frequently, you just don't have the focus, and it becomes a herculean task to get the darned thing done, and so it doesn't happen.

Excuse Number Two – "It costs too much."

Let's go back to our discussion of LCV—lifetime customer value—for a minute. I understand that a remodeler is going to have a different LCV from a painter, who is going to have a different LCV than a pool and spa contractor or a roofer. But I'm going to say that LCV will be at least $2,000 for any contractor—and could be as high as $100,000 or more.

My question to you is this: If customers are worth even $2,000 in profits to you on average, is it worth investing twenty-five dollars a year to stay on their radar?

Look, keeping your customers happy and staying top of mind with them is a *marketing investment*. You cannot look at it as an operational expense. You should be willing to spend *at least* as much to keep a customer as you would to attract a new customer.

Let's not have any more talk about it being too expensive.

Excuse Number Three – "I'm a really bad writer."

Well, if you follow the formula I recommend, you won't have to do much writing at all. I think you'll find, as many have, that it's not as difficult as you think it is.

I like to write the way I talk. You should do the same. There's even software now that will transcribe what you say, so you can simply talk your entire newsletter. What could be easier than that?

**Excuse Number Four – "Can't I just e-mail it?
It would save so much money."**

E-mail is a great way to communicate with your customers, and I encourage you to use e-mail and social media to increase the number of times you touch your customers. But it's not the same as sending them something in the mail.

The problem is that people are bombarded by e-mail. In the account that I use for my family e-mail, I get two hundred e-mails a day. I'll bet your customers get about the same number. There's a good chance that your e-mail will either hit their spam folders, or it'll just get deleted without being read.

But when people get a letter in their mailbox, it's a different story. When they hold the newsletter in their hand, you make a personal connection with them. And that newsletter may sit on their coffee table for a while, where other family members can read it. If you're really lucky, it'll end up in the bathroom, where people have time to read your interesting stories and articles.

Use this strategy correctly, and you will build your own glass wall around your clients, get them to refer more often, and move your bottom line up quickly.

As an aside, I think the fitness business I spoke of earlier is making a huge mistake by relying on e-mail alone. If they asked me, I would strongly advise them to add a printed newsletter to their arsenal.

**Excuse Number Five – "I don't have time." Or,
"I have too much to do already."**

This is the number one excuse I hear for not doing a monthly mail program.

The only answer I can give you is that you'll need to make time. Remember, we're talking about your most valuable asset. Protecting your customer base is crucial.

Go ahead and get the template that I have for you on the website. It's free, and I promise you'll discover that a monthly mailing program isn't that hard to do after all. Once again, the website is www.bernieheer.com.

Don't discount the power of a mail program. If you told me I could keep only one marketing strategy, this is the one I would keep. Absolutely no doubt about it.

80/20 Sales and Marketing

Before we move on from this topic, I want to touch on something called the 80/20 principle and what it means to you and your business.

You've probably heard of 80/20: 80 percent of your profits come from 20 percent of your customers…or 80 percent of your problems come from 20 percent of your customers…or 20 percent of your effort generates 80 percent of your results…and so forth.

But there's much more to 80/20 than meets the eye. In his recent book, *80/20 Sales and Marketing*—a book you should read—author Perry Marshall explores how 80/20 can give you incredible insights into your business.

He's got a great website set up at www.8020curve.com, and you can play with all kinds of very interesting numbers. You don't even need to put in your e-mail to use it.

For instance, let's say that you're a remodeler, and you have done 250 projects for 250 different customers. Let's also say that the average project was $35,000. Here's just some of what we can learn from 80/20:

- 31 customers would spend $50,000 with you.
- 14 customers would spend $100,000 with you.
- 8 customers would spend $150,000 with you.
- 6 customers would spend $200,000 with you.
- 2 customers would spend $400,000 with you.
- 1 customer would spend $600,000 with you.

That's kind of cool, isn't it? It proves that there's money waiting to be taken from these customers if only you would offer them an opportunity to spend it with you. In fact, there's $3.55 million dollars sitting there in your customer base just waiting for you to go and get it.

How about the other way?

- 92 customers would spend $20,000 with you.
- 129 would spend $15,000.
- 206 would spend $10,000.

Wow! That tells you that a bunch of your customers are ready to give you more money if you'd come up with an offer at a price point lower than what you already did for them.

One note...the numbers for the lower spending amount tend to be less accurate than the numbers moving up the scale. When I put in $5,000, the program told me that all 250 customers would spend that amount. Well, that's unreasonable, as I'm sure you can see. (What this number is actually telling us is that, in your *prospect* pool, there are lots of people who will spend $5,000 with you for *something*...You just need to make the offer.)

These numbers make a very compelling case for a contractor to continually offer customers options and ways for them to spend money with you—both at a higher price point and a lower price point than your average project.

But, in order to make these offers, you need to maintain your relationship with them.

CHAPTER 14

The Magic of Marketing Systems

Is there one thing you can do—one activity you can add to your schedule—that will dramatically impact your business and financial success?

There is...and that activity is planning.

I placed this chapter before the one about strategies to double or triple your business because, once you read that chapter, you're going to be so excited to start implementing that you'll forget about the systems you need to manage all that activity.

Don't worry, though, this chapter is short.

Many years ago I decided it would be cool to get my pilot's license. At the time I lived in Charlotte, North Carolina, and I found a tiny little airport in Monroe, North Carolina, that offered flying lessons. This place was so small that they rented part of their land to a chicken farm, and when the wind was coming our way, the smell was horrible.

I took about twenty hours of lessons in a Cessna 152. I loved it but quickly realized that flying is a very expensive hobby. I got as far as my first solo cross-country flight—that's where the student flies solo to three different airports at least fifty miles apart. It was thrilling to be up there all by myself piloting my little plane.

Shortly after that, my company said they wanted me to open a sales office in Raleigh, North Carolina, which is about a three-hour drive from Charlotte. I took the job and moved, and that was the end of my flying lessons. I never did take it up again.

Anyway, one thing I remember very clearly from my flying lessons is that taking off is the easy part...Landing is the hard part.

You see, when you're coming in for a landing, you have to position the plane at the right altitude to come in smoothly. You have to factor in the wind, which is trying to blow you off course. And you're flying slowly—oftentimes using flaps to increase lift and allow slower speed—so the stall warning is blaring away to alert you that you are about to stall the airplane and crash.

It's nerve-racking because there's so much going on and so many things to keep track of.

So it is with marketing. Taking off—implementing strategies—is the easy part. Landing—handling the increased phone activity, collecting prospect and client information, tracking the effectiveness of each campaign, scheduling prospect appointments, preparing proposals, and more—that's the hard part.

The last thing I want is for you to be overwhelmed by the activity created from the new marketing that you decide to do and be sorry that you ever did it.

We're going to do some *backwards* thinking by preparing ahead of time to handle the results of your marketing efforts.

In order to manage the new activity, you need to have some simple systems in place. I'm not saying that you need to invest in expensive new software or have an elaborate process. All I'm talking about is a piece of paper or an Excel file with some specific information.

I'm going to recommend three systems:

1. A system to manage your marketing campaigns
2. A system to manage your leads
3. A system to manage client relationships

Managing Your Marketing Campaigns

One of the key things you'll want to do is to keep track of how well your marketing campaigns are working. We're going to go through a number of ideas in the next chapter, but let's say you decide to try four new marketing strategies.

You'll want to create a spreadsheet listing all of your marketing campaigns—the four new ones as well as any you already had going, like Yellow Pages.

When a lead comes into your business, one of the initial questions you'll ask is how the caller found out about you. Keep track of the number of leads you get from each marketing strategy, and you'll soon see which ones are generating more leads and which are generating fewer leads. During a power hour, you can calculate the cost per lead and start to get a good sense as to how much it's costing you for a lead from each marketing strategy.

Managing Your Leads

Let's say that your sales process has five steps:

1. A prospect calls, and you or your staff collect information from the caller.
2. You send or e-mail information to them.
3. You meet with them to discuss their project and collect information you need to prepare your proposal.

4. You deliver the proposal and seek to close the sale.
5. You follow up if they didn't become a client.

Of course, a custom home builder or a pool and spa contractor—where the project is more complex, and design is going to come into play—will have more steps. A painter, roofer, or paving contractor may combine steps three and four.

In any case, you'll want to create a spreadsheet to track each prospect to make sure that you've covered each step. On the spreadsheet, in addition to information about where they are in the sales process, you'll want to include information about where the leads came from so that you can track which lead sources are generating prospects that ultimately hire you. This step is overlooked by so many contractors, and it's critically important.

Managing Client Relationships

You may believe that this is an operational matter and not a marketing matter, but I disagree. I believe that you need to continue marketing to clients during the project and even after the project. They need to feel appreciated, and they need to know that you care about them in order to refer to you in the future and to be references for you.

Depending again on the complexity of your typical project, you may have a basic set of steps in your head, or you may use project-management software to keep track of all the various aspects of a project.

My recommendation is that you think about and add in some steps that are designed specifically to keep the customer engaged, informed, and happy. When customers don't know what's happening, they become anxious. Anxious customers are not happy. It's most often a matter of communicating with them.

So, build steps into your process to remind yourself to call or leave a note for a customer at certain points during each project. Even if you're a chimney sweep and all of your projects are completed within a few hours, it would make your customers much more appreciative if you would call them after you're done to let them know, and reassure them that their chimney is in good shape.

I have prepared samples of these three spreadsheets for you. You can get them for free at www.bernieheer.com.

These three simple systems will enable you to stay on top of all of the activity and make sure that all prospects and customers are getting the attention they deserve. And it'll keep you from going crazy.

SECTION IV
Applying Upside-Down, Inside-Out, and Backwards Marketing Methods

CHAPTER 15

The "Backwardest" (and Best) Advice I Can Give You

In this section, we'll jump into the specific strategies to boost your revenues and profits.

I'd like to start by giving you the strategy that was the inspiration for this book. This is the original idea that had other marketing "experts" accusing me of giving backwards advice.

I call this my "backwardest" advice. As you might guess, it's very logical and makes perfect sense. Here it is: **fix your sales process before you start doing lead generation.**

You know, it's funny. The hundreds and hundreds of businesses that I've consulted with all started out in pretty much the same place…They had reasonably good lead flow, but they weren't getting many of the jobs they bid on.

In fact, most were closing only about 20 percent of their proposals, or one out of five.

That means four out of five prospects hired someone else. That's an awful lot of time put into preparing and presenting proposals, most of which never paid off.

And if you ask most marketing or business consultants…they'll tell you that you need to increase lead flow.

They'll tell you to get a bigger Yellow Pages ad, do targeted direct mail, join a networking group, optimize your website, get a Facebook page, start a social media campaign, and on and on.

Just get more leads…and your problems will be solved.

Now, I'm the first to admit that lead flow is the lifeblood of every contracting business. There's no arguing that if you get more leads, you will almost certainly get more business.

But wouldn't increasing your leads also mean a lot *more* time and energy wasted preparing and presenting proposals? And still only one in five will turn into sold business.

What if, instead of increasing lead flow, we instead focus on your closing ratio? What would that look like?

We need to do a little math here, but stick with me…This'll be really quick. You'll see in just a second how important it is to grasp these numbers. Quite frankly, this is going to change your life.

Let's say that your company gets twenty leads a month, you close 20 percent of those leads (one in five), you land four jobs per month, and you have $1 million in revenue a year.

That's where you are today…right now. Here's what that looks like:

Annual Leads	Current Closing Ratio	Jobs Landed	Average Sale	Annual Revenue
100	20%	20	$50,000	$1 Million

Now, you work on your sales process so that you're closing more sales, and next month, here's what your numbers look like:

Annual Leads	Current Closing Ratio	Jobs Landed	Average Sale	Annual Revenue
100	30%	30	$50,000	$1.5 Million

Same one hundred leads coming in...but your closing ratio is now 30 percent instead of 20 percent, so you land thirty jobs instead of twenty.

Notice that you *didn't* have to do a lot more work to prepare and deliver any more proposals, but you generated $500,000 more in revenue!

It's like magic. By increasing your closing ratio only ten points, you bump your revenue by 50 percent—and that adds up to half a million dollars!

That's a lot of money. And, I would argue, it's very profitable revenue because you didn't have to add overhead expenses like insurance or buy any more tools and equipment. You may not even need to add manpower.

Think about what you would do with that money...

Would you get a new truck? Would you finally pay yourself a decent wage? Start a 401(k) plan so that you can quit working at some point down the road? Maybe take a dream vacation with your family?

This math works up and down the scale.

If you were making $500,000...you're now making $750,000.

If you were making $5 million...you're now making $7.5 million.

That's the reason I recommend that you work on your closing ratio first. The only time you would work on your lead flow first is if you have no leads at all coming in. Even then, it might make more sense to figure out your sales process before launching a big push for leads.

We can all agree that doing some *backwards thinking* and focusing on your closing ratio just makes sense. You can start making more money right away without creating a lot of additional work for yourself.

Don't Be Lazy about This!

Since 2002, I've been pushing and prodding contractors to work on their sales processes to improve their closing ratios. I've heard every excuse why they can't or won't do it.

"My salespeople won't use the system."

The best salespeople are usually motivated by one thing—making sales. Whether for the thrill of hearing the word "yes" or the money they make when they get a deal, this is their motivation.

In my experience, they are willing to follow any process or system that will mean more yesses and more money for them.

Perhaps, at some point, you've paid for sales training and didn't see much impact. Sales trainers—who are oftentimes really just motivational speakers—tend to get people all fired up with ideas. Once the salespeople get back to their desks, though, the excitement quickly wears off, they turn back to their old ways, and there's no lasting value from the sales training.

I'm not talking about sales training. I'm talking about honest-to-goodness tools that they can see and touch and hold in their hands that will dramatically impact their sales success.

"I'm too busy...I don't have time."

The best answer I can give you to this one is...make time. It's important.

If you invest just a few hours for three or four weeks, you'll save incredible amounts of time moving forward from there.

It just makes sense that if you can stop spending hours and hours preparing and delivering proposals that don't turn into sold business, you'll save yourself untold hours of time.

One way or another, you need to get this done.

"I don't have any sales training…I wouldn't know where to start."

Here's the best part: I have solved this problem for you.

I've written an e-book called *The 8 Essential Truths of Selling for Contractors* that outlines a simple, tested selling process that has bumped the closing ratios up to 40 percent, 50 percent, even 80 percent (or higher!) for the contractors who are using it.

The book outlines my step-by-step process that can be customized and implemented in your business in as little as twenty-seven days. Some have done it even more quickly than that.

Please visit the website for this book at www.bernieheer.com to get the book and discover how you can use the system in your business.

If you don't apply any of the other strategies in this book, you will still be well served if I succeed in getting you to work on your sales process. That's where the path to your financial freedom starts.

CHAPTER 16

Creative Strategies to Double or Triple Your Business

I'm guessing this is the chapter you've been waiting for.

If you looked at the table of contents and opened to this chapter...welcome! I strongly recommend that you go back and read from chapter 1. Without the core thinking behind these strategies, you aren't likely to have success with them. You will have much more success if you read the whole book.

Besides, reading the earlier chapters won't take that much time.

I've addressed direct mail and online marketing—two critical marketing strategies that every contractor should be using—elsewhere in this book, so I am not going to talk about them again here. The strategies in this chapter are those that are a little different and creative.

In this chapter, I'm going to give you a number of specific strategies that are designed to get the phone ringing with prospects that are eager to work with you.

To paraphrase an old saying, "I don't know one strategy to get you a hundred new customers, but I know a hundred ways to get one customer."

Most business owners are looking for that one thing they can do to improve their business, make more money, close more sales, work less and make more, and retire wealthy.

I'm sorry to tell you that there is no one thing that'll make all of that happen. Not even the Internet.

You'll need to pick four to six strategies and implement them at the same time. That's sometimes called "taking massive action."

Of the four or six, two or three will work well for you, the others… maybe not so well. Some may take a little while to begin really working well. If needed, you'll come back here and pick a few more strategies and try those. Continue until you have the right number of leads, prospects, and customers flowing into your business every week or month.

It's important to have more than one lead source. Businesses that were dependent on broadcast fax or telemarketing as their lead-generation source were put out of business when these marketing methods were suddenly banned. Businesses that depend on e-mail marketing are quickly losing ground as people ignore more and more of their e-mails.

If one of your marketing methods suddenly stops producing for some reason, it's not a big deal. You'll simply try two or three new ones until you figure out how to replace that one.

Take Control of Your Lead Generation

Building your own lead-generation machine has incredible power. You get to decide how big or how small you want your business to be, which projects you want to do and which you want to turn away, who you want to work with and who you don't. You'll have the kind of freedom you've only dreamed about.

Plus, having some complexity in your systems will keep your competitors perplexed. It's unlikely that they will do even half of the things that you do to generate new sales, which is going to pay huge dividends to you.

As we talk about these strategies, please keep in mind that ordinary marketing delivers ordinary results. This goes back to doing the same thing everyone else is doing. If you want better-than-mediocre results, you need to do something different. You'll find that a lot of my strategies are different.

Resist the temptation to cast aside any strategy because you don't think you want to do it. Think about how you can adapt the idea to your business so that you're comfortable with it. It might just turn out to be the best strategy of all for you.

And let me know what works for you. I want to hear about your successes.

So let's jump in. Some of these methods have been mentioned elsewhere in this book, but I'm going to touch on them again here.

The Number One Way to Double Your Business

Doubling your business is simple. Just get every client to refer one new customer.

I know, I know…sounds simple, but how do you do it?

DM News recently said, "Consumers trust recommendations above all other forms of advertising. They're more willing to buy based on a friend's endorsement even if they've never heard of the vendor or seller before."

You must find a way that you're comfortable with to make referrals a part of your business. I'm going to give you some ideas.

Start by making it clear to customers—both past and present—that you want and expect referrals. When a customer says something nice like, "Wow, I really love how the tile you recommended turned out. It really looks great," make it a habit to reply, "Thanks. I'd really appreciate it if you tell anyone you know who might be looking to have a project like this done how pleased you are with our work."

Take that line, change it so that you're comfortable with it, and practice it over and over until it comes out as natural and easy as saying hello.

Next, create a referral reward program. And please don't cheap out on this. Remember our discussion about lifetime customer value.

If you're a custom home builder, a remodeler, or a pool contractor, you can certainly afford a referral reward valued in the $500 to $1,000 range. That's a whole lot more than any of your competitors are giving away for a referral. I like to offer three rewards so that clients can choose which one they want.

A painter, paving contractor, roofer, or similar type of contractor probably can't afford that level, but $150 to $200 is doable. There are a lot of great things you can get for that kind of money, especially electronics. And, again, your competitors—if they do anything—are giving twenty-five-dollar gift cards.

If you can arrange with another local business to package a reward, you can "plus" the value of the referral reward. For instance, a dinner for four at a nice restaurant would be a very nice referral reward. But, if you approach the owner and arrange for the dinner to be on a Tuesday or Wednesday—typically slow nights—then you might get the dinner at a pretty nice discount. Plus, the restaurant is potentially getting people in the door that they wouldn't have gotten otherwise, so the discount they're giving you is really a marketing expense for them.

One note: if you do arrange a dinner as a referral reward, specify that it comes with a bottle of wine with your compliments. Otherwise, the party might go through several bottles of expensive wine and expect you to pay the tab. Don't ask me how I know…

I would suggest that you put together a tiered reward program: a more modest reward for a single referral, and a much nicer reward for people who refer, say, three or five people to you.

You want to reward everyone who refers, whether you end up getting the job or not. So I suggest a simple "thank you for the referral" gift as soon as you get a referral. I've always preferred gifts that took just a little thought and effort, like a movie and an ice cream for two, but it could be just a gift card to Dunkin' Donuts or Starbucks. When you get the job, then you give the referrer the bigger reward.

Finally, everyone who refers gets put into two drawings. Once a month you pick a client of the month who gets a nice prize, and once a year, someone gets picked for a big-screen TV or some other really nice thing.

I know this sounds complex, but it's very simple to keep track of referrals. And think of it from the customers' point of view…To them it seems like someone's always winning something, and they will want to be part of the action.

The Power of Endorsement

Endorsements can take many shapes. These aren't quite as strong as referrals, but you cover a lot more ground with endorsements. You're hoping to get your name in front of people who are looking for a contractor like you but wouldn't otherwise hear about you or be referred to you.

They can be a huge shortcut to entering a new target market.

When I started my first business back in 1998, I tried to get clients by cold calling. It was a miserable failure. I made 2,437 calls in the course of two and a half months and got one client…a small one. I knew I had to find a better way.

Luckily I had maintained a relationship with a very successful insurance broker that I'd done business with when I was a company rep. He and I worked out an arrangement where he would send twelve letters a week to his clients, and I would follow up with them.

Suddenly the doors were open, and I got twenty or so clients very quickly. In fact, some of the people who had refused to see me when I cold called now welcomed me and were even relieved that I was able to help them. It was the start I needed to get my business rolling.

Endorsements can make all the difference.

Earlier I mentioned that you should call everyone and anyone that you're a client of—your accountant, your insurance brokers and agents, your dentist, and so forth—and buy them breakfast to show them the kind of work you do.

What I suggest to plus this strategy is that you create a special offer for their clients. And, in addition to that, you can describe your referral reward program and tell them that they're eligible for the referral rewards. Ideally you would like for these people to offer to send a letter to their client bases describing your business and your special offer. But, even if this doesn't happen, you will have gotten the "inside out" about your company.

Also in an earlier chapter, I mentioned the idea of partnering with a theater group, an opera house, or a performing arts center to offer them either free or discounted services in exchange for their endorsement. I won't go through that again, but it's a great way to establish your presence in a target market.

Another idea for you is to get a group of like-minded business owners together—say six to eight—and set up a cross-promotion. It works like this: Let's say your group consists of a painter, a roofer, a home remodeler, a plumber, an auto mechanic, an electrician, and a landscaper. All members of the group would have a packet of material about the others that would be left with each customer they see.

Obviously, the auto mechanic's packet wouldn't have his own information, just the information about the others, and your packet wouldn't have your own information.

This can be set up as a simple recommendation, "These are other contractors and service providers we know and recommend," or each member of the group can come up with a special offer for the customers of the other members.

As the organizer, the other members will probably look to you to help put their offers and material together. It might take a little time, but it'll be well worth the effort.

Another form of endorsement is to ask customers who are pleased with your work if you can send a letter to their neighbors mentioning that you did work at their home. This is oftentimes called a "champion."

The key here is that *you're* going to do all the work. So you simply write a short letter that describes what you did for the customer and how pleased they are with the outcome. It's critical to get a testimonial from the customer and include that in the body of the letter.

Then, if you can get a neighborhood directory from the customer, simply send the letter to all the homes, personalized, of course. A directory of their church or temple members would work equally well. If there is no neighborhood directory, then I suggest you look into the postal service's Every Door Direct Mail process, which lets you send a mailer to every address on a specific carrier's mail route. It's comparatively inexpensive, but there are some limitations on what you can send.

Imagine…once you've started to work in a specific market, each time you send out an endorsement letter, some of the same people will be getting another letter. Do you think they'll want to speak to you when they're ready to undertake a project? You bet they will! You just have to be a little careful not to make every letter the same.

Be sure to give champions credit for their referrals, and reward them just as if they had referred someone directly to you. If you get five new customers from an endorsement mailer, you might want to go and see your champion and find out whether he or she would prefer a nice trip or a big-screen plasma TV instead of five of your regular referral rewards.

Angie's List, HomeAdvisor, and all the others are a subtle form of endorsement. I would even add Yelp, Google Places, and the other directories where people can leave ratings, as endorsement platforms. It's important that you monitor what's happening on these sites and that you do all you can to control comments and rankings.

Your employees can also be endorsement partners of sorts. Ask your employees to make a list of people they know in the community. You'll have to prompt them to think of people they know in their neighborhoods, through their churches or temples, through the PTA, through their kids' sports or activities, through clubs they might belong to, and so forth.

Let your employees know that you would like them to send a letter to these people telling them about your company and the type of work that you do. Of course, you'll write the letter, print it up, and send it out, but it will be from them and have their signature at the bottom of it.

One last idea for you on endorsements: approach a business that has the same customer base as you do—meaning the same target market. This could be a high-end appliance store, a luxury auto dealership, a nice menswear store, a salon, a fine furniture store, or other type of business. Offer to put on a seminar for their customers in their showroom. Give the seminar a compelling title like "Six Great Ways to Freshen Up Your Home's Look That'll Make You the Envy of the Neighborhood."

The benefit for them is that they get people into their store or showroom, and they are offering their customers something of value. It's a reason to be in contact with their customers, which is always good. And, if they're smart, they'll have some nice refreshments for them, or even arrange for a wine or chocolate tasting with a third or fourth business in town.

You can let them know that you'll send information about the event to your own customer list, so it'll be an opportunity for them to attract more new clients as well.

You'll most likely have to write the invitation that will be sent to their customer list, but that's actually what you want, because you then control the content.

An alternative to this approach is that each of you will send a mailer to your lists endorsing the other. So you mail to your list about a nice restaurant—you can even do it as an insert in your newsletter, which will cost you almost nothing—and they mail to their list about you. Each follows up shortly thereafter to the other's list with an offer or follow-up.

Always keep your eyes open for endorsement opportunities. If done correctly and consistently, these can be a major source of new business for you, and the cost and effort aren't overwhelming.

Maintain Your Relationships

I focused on this topic in chapter 13, so I won't spend a lot of time on it here. But this is so important that I want to mention it again.

Your printed and mailed newsletter is the key to maintaining your relationships with your customers. Now you can add to your mailing list the names of the people who you got from your endorsements as well. The more the merrier!

You'll use your newsletter to let people know about your referral reward program, and specials you're offering, and other events you have going on. You'll also use your newsletter to announce the customer of the month and the winners of any prizes.

Seasonal greetings are a great way to touch your customers more frequently, and you want to do these in addition to your newsletter. I tend to steer away from greetings around the December holidays because your card is going to get lost in the huge pile of cards that many people get.

Think about other holidays and messages you could use:

Thanksgiving – *I'm thankful for customers like you…*

Valentine's Day – *I LOVE my customers…*

St. Patrick's Day – *I'm the luckiest guy in the world…*

Fourth of July – *I'm seeing fireworks…*

I recently got a gift from the AdWords guru Perry Marshall—I'm in a mastermind group that he runs. It's a little gizmo that attaches to anything and turns it into a speaker. You can stick it to a table, a box, a coffee mug, anything…and it's a speaker. Very cool.

I was thrilled to get it. It's not especially expensive, but as they say, it's the thought that counts.

Constantly be on the lookout for new ways you can stay in touch with your customers and prospects.

Yellow Pages Advertising

I think it's a mistake to abandon the Yellow Pages. Although I personally haven't consulted the Yellow Pages in quite a while, I know there is a substantial population out there who still does. And they are often the people with the money.

The baby boom generation is much less likely than younger generations to use the Internet. These folks have the lion's share of wealth in the United States, and ignoring them is a mistake. It's a fact that the wealthier a person is, the less likely they are to be constantly connected, whether it's through Internet, texting, or using social media.

These are the folks who still read books, get their magazines delivered by the postman, use their phones to talk to people, and "let their fingers do the walking."

The strategy in the Yellow Pages is to have an ad that looks very different than everyone else's there. It's a very competitive environment because everybody in your section is offering the same services that you are. It's hardly optimal.

Look back at chapter 11, where we talked about copywriting strategies. I suggest that you write an ad that looks more like a sales letter than a typical Yellow Pages or newspaper ad. And be sure it has a compelling headline. This will stand out from every other ad and will attract eyes as a result.

A side benefit is that you can probably use a smaller, less expensive ad than you may have used in the past. And, by the way, Yellow Pages reps will fight you and tell you that your ad won't work. Ignore them. Or better yet, ask them whether they ever tried an ad like that and what the results were.

Like any other media, you'll need to decide what action you would like people to take when they read your YP ad. Do you want them to call your office? Do you want them to get your consumer information report? Do you want them to go to your website? Direct readers to take the action that you want them to take.

As for which book to be in, that's a tough one to figure out. One HVAC contractor had his phone staff ask all callers what book they use. After a few weeks, it was clear which one was the most used in his city.

Bump and Upsell

This topic almost deserves a whole chapter to itself. In chapter 13, I went through some numbers using the 80/20 principle that showed how many of your customers would spend more with you if you only offered them the opportunity to do so.

In this part, I want to talk about how to do that.

You may recall the annual fishing trip I take with my two brothers. This year will be the ninth year that we're doing that trip. Every year I contact the boat captain to arrange the date. And every year he just books the trip. He has never once offered me any kind of additional option that would get me to spend more money.

And the thing is…I would probably spend more money.

What could he offer me?

How about a breakfast basket with nice bagels and muffins, maybe some fruit? And some really good sandwiches and munchies for lunch. As it is, we stop at the 7-Eleven very early in the morning and pick up their prepackaged items before heading down to the dock at 5:30 a.m. I would definitely pay for nicer food and the convenience of not having to make the stop at 7-Eleven. I could get another half hour of sleep!

Because the day starts so early, I'm guessing most of his customers stay at a local hotel the night before. He could arrange a hotel-and-restaurant package for his customers that includes some nice extras that others don't usually get.

Think very carefully about your business, and put together offers for every customer at different price points. About 20 percent of people will go for a premium option if offered one. By not offering it, you are leaving money behind, or you may lose a job because another contractor did offer a premium or upgraded option.

Doing this also reduces the focus on price. If you offer a basic, deluxe, and premium option at three price points, most people will go for the middle option. The price-sensitive prospects may go for your basic service, but you may have lost them if you didn't offer it. The lower-cost option is generally going to be priced lower due to lower cost materials or fewer options, so you don't necessarily lose any profit on these jobs. And those that go for the premium option will be much more profitable for you.

I like to call this "choosing between you, you, and you."

A related strategy is called the upsell. In the upsell, you first close the deal, then seek to sell additional services or products. For instance, if you're a painter and you just got a job for four rooms, you could then offer the homeowner a big discount for additional rooms. It won't cost you much more to paint a fifth room, so you offer a very attractive price for each additional room.

Or, if you notice that the moldings and doors are in bad shape, you make an attractive offer to do a touch-up on these areas.

As you consider what you could offer, ask yourself, "What else would my clients like from me?"

If you're a home remodeler, when you get a kitchen remodel, offer a big discount on a bathroom remodel. Or offer an upgrade on the kitchen cabinets or countertop if the customer also does a built-in TV-and-shelving unit in the family room.

If you're a pavement contractor, make an offer to install a curb alongside the driveway, which will make it look really nice.

You get the idea. You are in a great position, once you have been selected for a project, to make offers for additional services. The customer generally has a very high opinion of you at this point in the relationship. You don't want to abuse that trust, but you should seize the opportunity.

Direct Mail

I know that direct mail is often viewed as a marketing strategy that's past its prime, and plenty of marketing people swear that it's a waste of money because—they think—everybody prefers to get e-mails and tweets. I disagree.

It might surprise you to learn that Internet-based companies like Amazon, eBay, and Google use direct mail. Why do you think that is? These are companies that understand web and e-mail marketing probably better than anyone else.

They use direct mail because it is profitable. And you should too.

Throughout this book we've talked about various ways to use direct mail, some perhaps not so obvious at first glance.

Your print newsletter is direct mail. Your seasonal greeting cards and postcards from your vacation are direct mail, as is an endorsed mailer. I even consider the "five-house plan" to be direct mail.

The five-house plan is the strategy where you leave your information with the five houses adjacent to the house you're working in. The mistake that most contractors make, by the way, is that they only put a door hanger on these homes. If you're going to take the time to use this strategy, why not write a personalized letter, including the name of the neighbors that you're doing work for, along with your consumer information?

All of these should be approached using the strategies I detailed in chapter 12 to create great ads.

Of course, when I say direct mail, most people think about postcards or letters sent to cold lists. If done properly, these can certainly work, and have been a mainstay of contractor marketing for a long, long time.

My recommendation is that you use these as a secondary marketing strategy if other strategies I've outlined for you don't work. You're much more likely to have success with a marketing strategy done as a "warm" approach, like an endorsed mailer or a referral.

If you decide to do mailers to cold lists, focus your mailer to a small target market that you've selected and for which you've specifically developed a message. You'll waste huge sums of money—and end up with customers you don't want—if you do a large mailer to "everyone and anyone."

Yard Signs

Yard signs are a proven and effective way to get quality prospects. One statistic I saw recently suggested that for home remodelers, 75 percent of their new customers came from yard signs. That's huge!

Yard signs—sometimes called jobsite signs—are a form of endorsement. Neighbors will assume that your customer did some amount of due diligence in selecting you, and you get instant credibility as a result.

Many custom home builders, home remodelers, pool and spa contractors, and landscape design contractors use yard signs. But what I see too often are the cheap, flimsy signs similar to those used by politicians at election time.

Do yourself a favor and build a decent yard sign. You are a contractor, after all. If you're a home remodeler or custom builder, use nice wood and molding to make it look like a professional built it. If you're a pool and spa contractor, build it out of PVC pipe. If you're a landscaper, build it out of old shovels and rakes.

On vacation recently, I saw a landscaper's yard sign that was a huge flower, with the petals made out of old shovel heads welded together. It was truly beautiful.

You get the idea. My brother, the plumber, took my advice and built his yard sign out of copper pipe. It's great…and eye-catching.

Now, roofers, painters, pavement contractors, and others—who tend to be on a jobsite for a much shorter period of time—are less likely to use yard signs. That's a mistake. While it's true that fewer people will see your sign in one yard, you'll have exposure to a larger audience because you might have your sign in multiple locations every week.

My brother, after getting permission from the homeowner, puts his sign out before he unpacks his tools. When he's done with the job and has packed up his truck, he removes the sign, and off he goes. He might have his sign in five or six spots every day! And he's gotten plenty of calls from people who saw his sign.

A couple of things to know about yard signs:

- Plan to put them up so that the sign is perpendicular to the street, with your information and message on both sides.
- Keep the message simple: your USP, your company name, the nature of the work you do (if it's not obvious from your company name), and your phone number.
- Use simple fonts and have high contrast between the lettering and the background.
- Be sure to get permission from the homeowner. Some homeowner associations don't permit signs in yards.

Networking Groups

Networking groups can work very well for contractors, but you have to know what you're getting into and what to expect.

First of all, when you're invited to join a networking group, first go to at least two meetings as a guest. What you're trying to figure out is how long the group has been in existence and what types of businesses are part of the group.

If the group is well established, has been active for a number of years, and has a solid number of members, then it may be a good fit for you. If a group is new and has only a few members—especially if it has only a few contractors—it might be best to look elsewhere.

Other contractors are your most likely source of referrals. Noncontractor members of the group might occasionally refer to you—or hire you themselves—but it's the members who are involved in the building trades that will usually be the most productive for you.

Networking groups are all about giving. You'll have to put the time in and give others referrals before you start to reap the rewards. It's not unusual to be part of a networking group for six to twelve months before a decent referral comes your way. And it might take two years or more before referrals really start rolling. Be patient, work the process, and your involvement will almost certainly pay off.

Publicity

This is another topic about which entire books and courses have been written, so I'm only giving you some of the highlights here.

Publicity can mean a number of different things: getting an article about you in the paper, writing a regular column for a magazine or newspaper, or having an article online that attracts someone seeking information.

The commonality is that they are free. Well, you don't pay for advertising, but it does require time, so they're not exactly free.

Let's start with getting an article written about you. The way to go about getting an article in a local newspaper—whether online or offline—is to submit a press release. The first thing to know is that a press release must follow a very specific format. I've posted a sample press release for you on this book's website at www.bernieheer.com, along with the rules for writing one.

As a contractor, you're most likely going to submit your press release to the editor of the "Home" section of your newspaper. Editors have a job to do, and it is to fill that section of the newspaper with interesting articles for the readers. They are always on the lookout for interesting articles, and sometimes they struggle to find material to fill their section.

This is a very important thing for you to know. You see, you're going to help the editors to do their job and fill their publication with fascinating articles. This is what you need to keep in mind when you write a press release. You have one goal: to get an article published. In order to accomplish that goal, you have to give the editors something that they can write a good article about.

What do you think this editor usually gets? Press releases that say, "Mark Jones Promoted to Sales Director" or "Smith Contracting Announces 15 Percent Increase in Sales." Boring!

You're going to give them something much better than that! Let's work on an example. Remember when we looked at the Giorgio letter and revised it so that a home-remodeling contractor could use it? Well, what if you took that concept and wrote a press release about it?

You start off with the headline for the press release, "Local Home Remodeler Takes On Role as Official Romance Director." Then, following the press release formula, you write a few short paragraphs about how women want to be pampered, how they need a personal space to escape the hustle-bustle of their day, and of course your service and offer.

Now the editors have something they can sink their teeth into. This is something different and much more interesting. If all goes according to plan, you will be interviewed, and an article will be written about you and your service, and it will appear in your local publication.

Articles and Columns

In the same way, articles and columns should provide interesting information related to your specialty, like what type of paint to use on different surfaces, how to keep your pool sparking clean all season, how to put up shelves, and easy repairs for small driveway cracks.

Take the articles directly to the editors or publishers of the local papers, particularly the local newspapers that are delivered to all households free of charge. They are always looking for local information to fill their papers.

Be sure to tell them that you want a byline at the top of the column or article, and a sentence at the end that gives your company name, address, phone number, and website.

If you're a regular advertiser in these newspapers, they will likely include your column or article in their papers.

What about a newspaper column of your own? You've seen doctors and mechanics have them, why not you? In your column, you would answer questions from readers.

How do you benefit from a newspaper column? First of all, when you have your own column, you are considered the expert. Think about Lou Manfredini. His books have propelled him to the highest level of authority and expertise.

For years I've seen a remodeler have his own column in my local paper. He answers "tricky" problems that people have written in about. Everyone thinks he is the brightest and best remodeler there is, and he gets tons of business this way.

Plus you could use this in all your marketing materials. When you deliver a proposal, you could include copies of all the articles or columns you've written. Do you think this would help you establish credibility? Absolutely.

Now, I'll admit that it might be more difficult to write a weekly column as a painter, roofer, or pavement contractor since you don't have the variety of topics to write about that a landscaper, remodeler, or builder would. For you, I recommend that you focus on articles. Make it a regular part of your marketing plan to submit articles to your local newspaper. New product innovations or industry news could be topics, as long as you can put an interesting angle on them. Keep your eyes open for opportunities.

How do you get a newspaper column of your own? First, you have to really want one. It takes a commitment of time to write a column every week or every month. Don't do this if you aren't completely sure that you're willing to devote the time to do it well.

If you've decided you want to do it, simply call the editor of the newspaper and tell him or her your idea. If you're going to solicit questions from readers, then that's your concept. If you have another idea for a column, then you'll explain that to the editor.

Let him or her know specifically how the newspaper will benefit; explain how the readers will benefit from your column.

If the newspaper editor isn't interested, try a different publication. Many localities have a luxury publication that comes out once a month or so. You've probably been called to advertise in it.

Follow up and be persistent.

Business Card Advertising

Your business card should be a mini-advertisement.

Too many business cards list only name, rank, and serial number. They could be doing so much more.

First off, your business card should be full color and professionally designed. A graphic artist will do the design work for a very reasonable charge, and you can use the design over and over again. As an alternative, the large office-supply stores have business card design services available on their websites. Simply pick a design, upload your logo, add your information, and they'll print them and send them off to you.

Include your unique selling proposition. Go back to chapter 3 if you need a refresher on USPs. Essentially, this statement tells a prospect why you're different than any of your competitors. If you have a longer USP, then think about either shortening it for your business card or putting it on the back of your card.

Make your telephone number big and bold. I've seen so many business cards that have the phone number buried somewhere in tiny print. Don't make it difficult for your prospect to call you.

On the reverse side of the card, make an offer. If you've written a consumer education piece, then you want to let people know what it is and how they can get it. You could also use a mini-version of your Yellow Pages ad. Imagine that someone looking for your services happens to find one of your cards; is there something on the card that will sell that person on contacting you?

My last bit of advice on business cards is to make them legible. Skip the fancy lettering and the stock artwork (the hammer and saw, the paint can and brush, the ladder, etc.). Use the space to make your case as to why someone looking at the card should hire you.

There are many, many more strategies that you can use to build your business. I've given you those that I know will work if you implement them. Most are focused on referrals or endorsements because these have been proven to work best.

In the final chapter, I'll give you the one strategy that's the real secret to your success.

CHAPTER 17

The Key to Your Success

I n "Garden Song" by John Denver, there's a line that goes, "Man is made of dreams and bones."

So true.

I want you to accomplish every one of your dreams.

In this last chapter, we're going to talk about the one master key to success. And, yes, *upside-down, backwards, and inside-out thinking* applies here as well.

Before we get to the master key, though, we need to have a somewhat difficult conversation. I'm afraid that, if we don't talk about this, you'll end up getting very little real value from this book. Nothing will change for you.

As I said earlier, research and studies show that 85 percent of your success depends on mind-set—meaning attitude—and 15 percent on ability. Yet our educational system puts 85 percent of the emphasis on learning specific skills and only 15 percent on mind-set.

We need to turn it upside down.

Your mind-set is the most difficult and least tangible facet of building your business, but it's the most important. This is where you need to focus 85 percent of your effort.

Let me ask you a question...How much success do you deserve? Do you deserve to make $100,000 a year? $250,000? $500,000? $1 million? More?

So many people—contractors especially, I find—undervalue themselves. You may see yourself in your own mind as a $50,000-a-year person. Very few people ever break through those self-imposed limits. They subconsciously reject opportunities for greater success even when those opportunities are placed right in front of them.

The remedy is surprisingly simple. If you diligently follow a few steps—and have the self-discipline to stick with them—then you can break the cycle of negative self-image and achieve true success.

Here are the steps:

1. Set meaningful goals.
2. Make the decision to invest in resources and processes that will lead you to your goals.
3. Manage yourself and your time effectively.
4. Spend your time with positive, energetic, supportive people.
5. Invest in your tools and equipment, your vehicles, your clothes, and other external things that impact your attitude.

I'm not pretending that this is going to be easy for you. But if you spend a power hour each day for the next three months focused on following these five steps, you will achieve much greater success than you've ever dreamed you would.

And that brings us to the master key.

I've given you a big clue already as to the master key. Let me give you a few more...

According to Elvis Presley, we need "a little less conversation, a little more action."

Walt Disney said, "The way to get started is to quit talking and begin doing."

Early on in this book, I told you a story about how I played trombone in school and the impact that had on my life, including my time in Germany as an abroad student.

I think there are some significant lessons to be learned from this story:

1. I *made the decision* to make a change in my life.
2. I got a coach (private teacher) who held me accountable.
3. I disciplined myself to devote time every day to improving my playing.
4. I joined a group of like-minded people who were positive but who also challenged and encouraged me.

And, as silly as it may sound, it changed my life in a very positive way.

Let's get back to the master key.

If you haven't figured it out yet, it's very simple: **take action**.

You see, no one makes money by learning, or even mastering, marketing strategies. Marketing know-how by itself has never made anyone a single dime.

Applying marketing know-how, though, has made many people wealthy and given them lifestyles of personal freedom.

If you take action on three to five of the strategies contained in these pages, then you'll be getting more referrals and more jobs in a short time.

You'll have a constant stream of income coming in on a daily basis. You'll be financially free. And you'll be making the kind of money that, at one time, you thought was impossible.

All the great ideas I've given you in this book are useless unless *you* do something. If you put this book aside and carry on as you have been, then nothing will change.

You'll continue to fight for the scraps left over from your competitors or those that have better marketing or business management processes.

You'll be stuck in the low-price battle, struggling to get jobs for cheapskate customers that think you charge way too much.

You'll never earn the respect and income that you deserve as a skilled professional in your field.

Is that what you want?

We both know that, unless you start now, you'll soon get caught up in your work or another project and will probably not use any of these powerful strategies. I don't want that to happen to you.

Delay is the deadliest form of denial.

Here's what I recommend:

1. For the next three months, dedicate one hour each day to your marketing. Be consistent and disciplined. Put it on your calendar right now. If you have to, get up an hour earlier.

2. Don't try to start everything at once. Pick a minimum of three strategies from this book and work on those. You may have so

much success with them that you won't have to do any more. Use your first hour to decide which strategies you'll try first. Seriously consider a monthly mailing program as one of these strategies. (Get a sample at www.bernieheer.com.)

3. Don't worry if something doesn't work. A guided missile reaches its target by figuring out it is off course and making corrections. Don't be afraid to try something. Stop doing it if it doesn't work.

4. Read success books by authors like Zig Ziglar, Napoleon Hill, Jim Rohn, and others.

5. Join a mastermind and coaching group where you can gather with like-minded contractors and business owners who will support and encourage you.

After you've implemented some of these ideas, I personally want to hear from you. I want to specifically know of your success. That's one of the biggest rewards to me...hearing from contractors all over the country telling me that my book changed their lives.

Again, you must take action. I really can't stress this enough. Just reading about these ideas doesn't make you a better marketer. This book is worthless to you unless you take action on what you've learned.

Although I tend to prefer amusing quotes from people like Yogi Berra and Will Rogers, my very favorite quote of all time is from Goethe, who said this:

The moment one definitely commits oneself, then Providence moves too. All sorts of things occur to help one that would never otherwise have occurred. A whole stream of events issues from the decision, raising in one's favor all manner of unforeseen incidents and meetings and material assistance, which no man could have dreamed would have come his way.

Whatever you can do, or dream you can do, begin it. Boldness has genius, power and magic in it. Begin it now.

I read this quote back in 1998 and made the decision, right then and there, to leave my job and start my own business. It has been a fantastic journey, and yes, many types of assistance have come my way that I could never have dreamed of.

So go out there, kick butt, make a lot of money, and scorch your competition. Don't forget to love your family. And please let me know about your triumphs.

I wish you spectacular success.

About the Author

Bernie Heer is a marketing performance consultant and strategic advisor to small businesses. He started his first business in 1998, and after beating his head against the wall and trying to figure out how to get clients and make money, a "chance encounter" led him to discover the hidden world of direct-response marketing. The ideas and methods changed the course of his business...and his life.

In 2011, he sold his business for a very healthy seven-figure sum. He has attained his goal of living a life of personal freedom, and his mission now is to show other small-business owners how to attain the same lifestyle for themselves.